ON

TURING

John Prager

WADSWORTH

™

THOMSON LEARNING

Australia • Canada • Mexico • Singapore • Spain
United Kingdom • United States

In loving memory of Sidney Prager

Printed in the United States of America
1 2 3 4 5 6 7 04 03 02 01 00

For permission to use material from this text, contact us:
Web: http://www.thomsonrights.com
Fax: 1-800-730-2215
Phone: 1-800-730-2214

For more information, contact:
Wadsworth/Thomson Learning, Inc.
10 Davis Drive
Belmont, CA 94002-3098
USA
http://www.wadsworth.com

ISBN: 0-534-58364-4

Contents

Preface

This is a book about one of the most brilliant and influential thinkers of the 20th century. The majority of the books in this series are about philosophers and have been written by philosophers, as is appropriate. Alan Turing, though, was a mathematician and pioneer computer scientist, and so I, as a mathematician-cum-computer scientist myself, was asked to write this book to convey the importance of Turing's contributions from the point of view of a practitioner of those fields.

The primary audience for this series in general and this book in particular are college students interested in gaining a grounding in the thoughts and influences of some of the deepest thinkers in history. However, this book should be informative to any lay person who is interested in learning about Alan Turing and how his work was on the one hand fundamental to the computerized physical world we live in today, and on the other to the on-going theoretical debate about what thinking and intelligence actually consist of. Since Turing was a mathematician, no such book would be complete without a few equations, but it should be stressed that the mathematics reproduced herein is self-contained and requires no advanced mathematical background on the part of the reader for its understanding.

This mathematics, in fact, might appear at first a little off-putting to those not used to it. Some of the concepts are admittedly very abstract, and the proofs downright weird. These proofs can seem to be nothing more than tricks, and the reader might end up feeling that he or she has been taken advantage of. One of the recurring features of these mathematical demonstrations is in the application of some process to itself. It is in this recursive or self-referential (as distinct from circular) reasoning that much power comes, and observing its use is somewhat of a window into the mind of the originator. There should really be nothing strange about this concept – after all, in some sense the mere act of a philosopher contemplating an act of reason is recursive. When I was a graduate student in the Cambridge lab run by Maurice V. Wilkes, one of Turing's college classmates and later co-pioneer of the computer era, I discovered, not though lectures but the culture in the Lab, that no large-scale computer program was deemed worth its salt unless it could be applied to itself. Thus programming language compilers could compile themselves, text editors could edit their own source code, interactive help systems could help the users in their own use, and so on. While this sentiment was never explicitly explained, it seemed clear it was a tacit expression of homage to Turing.

I owe a debt of gratitude to a number of people who, in various ways, directly or indirectly, have helped me write this book. By a fortunate fluke of timing I received my formal education at a time when the pioneers of the computer field had reached positions of prominence in the academic community, and I have been be privileged to have met and/or taken courses from a number of Turing's contemporaries, names such as Maurice Wilkes, David Wheeler, Donald Michie, and Oliver Selfridge. Closer to home and to the present, I wish to thank Ron Frank, Yael Ravin and my editor Dan Kolak, and to acknowledge the support and resources I've received from the IBM T.J. Watson Research Center. Finally, I must apologize to my wife Ellen for the many lonely evenings she has spent in my presence and thank her deeply for all her love, support and encouragement.

Introduction

Nobody has made a more profound impact on the field of computers and computing than Alan Turing. His impact was twofold: on the one hand in the invention and development of fundamental ideas which have enabled machines and programming to have reached the levels of sophistication we see today, and on the other to have stimulated debate which still rages on what constitutes intelligence, thinking and understanding. This is all the more remarkable considering that he died only a few years after the age of modern computing had gotten underway.

This book is not an attempt to tease out and micro-analyse Turing's views on the usual material found in philosophy texts, even the subjects he mentions in his writings. Turing talks about the soul, intuition, determinism and free will, but only in passing. Other great thinkers have devoted more of themselves to these subjects, and indeed their thoughts are invariably the only aspect of themselves they have left to us. Alan Turing, though, made concrete contributions, from his hugely important wartime cryptography work to laying the foundations for computer science, software design and artificial intelligence (AI). This is not to say he did nothing of interest to a philosopher. He made seminal contributions in the area of mathematical logic, specifically the subject of computability, and his "Turing test" for determination of intelligence has been the subject of large numbers of articles and much debate. Computability might seem to be a subject only of interest to computer scientists, but the issue of whether there is an answer to every well-formed problem has been of interest to philosophers since Leibniz. As far as intelligence and thought are concerned, these have been serious questions of interest to great thinkers for millennia, and can easily serve as a jumping-off point for the even deeper questions of what is consciousness or even life itself.

The chapters on Turing's work on machine intelligence contain a number of examples of real-life situations where some aspect of intelligence is required. These examples are not hard to come by because they are all around us, but the ones presented here were chosen to illustrate a particular point, either in support or as a challenge. The arguments on both sides of the question of whether machine intelligence is possible are all very believable, and it might be very instructive for the reader to try to reconcile the arguments on both sides of the coin. It might turn out that the coin has more than two sides.

The plan of this book is as follows. Chapter 1 contains a brief chronology of the important events in Turing's life. In Chapter 2 we consider the notion of computability and the fundamental contribution Turing made through his 1937 paper *On Computable Numbers*. This paper introduced the concept of the *Turing machine*, which is used to this day to represent the essence of a computable function. Turing built on the work of Gödel, who had exposed cracks in the shield of completeness that Hilbert had attempted to build around mathematics by showing that not all true statements in a consistent arithmetic system are provable. Turing himself showed, through what is commonly called the *halting problem*, that there is no general procedure that can be mechanically followed for deciding mathematical propositions. In Chapter 3 we see a very different side of Turing's contributions; far from the rarified atmosphere of mathematical logic was the very practical problem of deciphering enemy military transmissions. During World War II Turing led a group of English cryptographers who attacked the problem of deciphering the intercepted messages sent by German military operations and encoded by the infamous Enigma machine. The group at Bletchley Park worked by building their own simulation of the Enigma which if configured correctly could decode the encrypted messages. The German Enigma, though, was a moving target which caused the English group to require ever more sophisticated decoding machinery, which led to the *Colossus*, one of the contenders for the title of first electronic computer. After the War, Turing published a design for the *ACE*, a computer which was built several years later, but it was the design rather than the computer itself which is historically significant. This design incorporated several important advances, including self-modifying programs and subroutine hierarchies, which have been used extensively in programming systems ever since.

In Chapter 4 we look at the relationships between Turing's work and the new field of computational linguistics that his work helped to come into existence. Chapters 5 and 6 are devoted to the Turing Test, a kind of imitation game that Turing introduced in his 1950 paper *Computing Machinery and Intelligence*. Even though the computers of Turing's era were extremely primitive by today's standards, Turing could foresee the time when their capabilities would appear to be on a par with that of humans. The test that Turing proposed is a procedure for determining whether under suitably controlled conditions, an observer could tell through dialogue whether he was interacting with a human or a computer. Asking whether this test is a true test of intelligence immediately leads to the question of what intelligence actually is, and whether it is even theoretically possible to build an intelligent machine with the same thinking and understanding abilities as a human. We summarize Turing's contributions in Chapter 7.

One of the themes that recurs in this book, and indeed in the fields discussed herein, is that of *levels of representation* and *levels of understanding*. From Russell 100 years ago to Computer Science today, from Gödel to Artificial Intelligence, choosing the right level of representation has been found to be critical for success. Moreover, switching between levels is key to certain proofs, as Turing showed with his Universal Turing Machine, and is widely thought to be critical for understanding of higher brain functions.

Some words are in order about the terminology used here. The words *thinking, understanding* and *intelligence* are used almost interchangeably to denote that state of cognitive ability which average humans possess. To simplify the exposition, it is assumed that an organism, whether biological or mechanical, when capable of one is capable of all three. The terms *cognitive* and *sub-cognitive* are used to refer to two levels of mental activity that some might call *conscious* and *sub-conscious*. The word *conscious* is intentionally avoided because of the connection with the highly charged word *consciousness*. The question of what consciousness and awareness are is not only a very difficult one, but one which Turing did not address in his writings, and is outside the scope of this book.

1

Chronology

An excellent account of Turing's life is given in his biography[1] by Andrew Hodges. We provide here a very abbreviated chronology of the major events in his life.

Alan Mathison Turing was born on June 23, 1912 to Julius and Ethel Turing, in London England. He had one older brother, John. When 14, he entered the Sherborne School, a Public school[2] in Dorset, on the South coast of England. He made few friends, and had some difficulty adapting to the rigours of his environment. His initial academic performance was unexceptional, but he did better and better as the years passed. His strongest subjects were mathematics and science, particularly chemistry. He was especially interested in theories that had some practical effect in the world around him. Although there were occasional flashes of truly advanced thinking, it was not till his college years that he showed his true genius.

Turing applied for a scholarship at Trinity College, Cambridge, the former home of Isaac Newton, James Clerk Maxwell, Bertrand Russell and a considerable percentage of the country's Nobel Prize winners, a college that any aspiring mathematician or scientist would seek to enter. It was also the college of his grandfather, John. However, he failed in this quest, but won a scholarship at King's College, Cambridge, his second choice. This was probably fortunate in the end, since King's has a mild reputation for accommodating unorthodox lifestyles.

After his three years[3] he graduated with distinction and was elected a Fellow of King's, following his work on the Central Limit

Theorem in the field of probability. In the study of the field today his name is not associated with the theorem since Turing was not the first to derive it. However, his work was original since he was unaware of Lindeberg's proof, and the fellowship was duly awarded.

In the summer of 1935 he had his first encounter with the brilliant Hungarian mathematician John von Neumann, who was taking some time off from Princeton. It was at this time that Turing determined to visit Princeton. In 1936 he wrote the first of the arguably two most influential of his papers, *On Computable Numbers, with an Application to the Entscheidungsproblem*, concerning the essence of what is computable, and introducing the concept of Turing machine. He was beaten to publication by a paper from the American Alonzo Church, who derived an essentially equivalent result but by using a very different approach. Turing went to Princeton to work with Church, and earn his doctorate. While there, *On Computable Numbers* was published in the Proceedings of the London Mathematical Society, and he won the Procter Fellowship, thanks in part to a letter of recommendation from von Neumann. Turing had many opportunities to speak with the great man at Princeton, and von Neumann in turn came to admire Turing's ideas about mechanizing mathematical systems. The two men are widely held to be the two who have made the greatest conceptual advances in aid of modern computer design, but von Neumann didn't become seriously interested in computers until after becoming aware of Turing and his work. One might speculate how the two influenced each other.

Turing returned to England, and with the war approaching, joined the Government Code and Cypher school in Bletchley Park, Buckinghamshire. At the same time, he gave a lecture course at Cambridge. At Bletchley Park, he led the effort to decipher German military codes which were encoded by the Enigma machine. Previously, decoding work in Britain had been the purview of classicists, but he and others established approaches firmly rooted in mathematics. Turing did original work in statistics to assist in the process. Machines were built to do the decoding, and while they could be considered early computers, especially the Colossi, they were used for a single purpose. This work strengthened in Turing a desire to build a general-purpose computer. While at Bletchley he nearly became formally engaged to a female colleague, but backed out.

In 1942 he went back to the US to act as a liaison with the American code-breaking effort. He spent time at Bell Labs working on the encipherment of speech, and met with the communication theorist Claude Shannon. He started his own speech encipherment work on return to England. In 1945 at the end of the war he joined the National Physical Laboratory in Teddington and started work on his own computer project, the ACE.

Turing found it difficult to deal with the organizational inertia of peacetime government bureaucracy. In 1947 he returned to Cambridge and the next year went to Manchester University to join the Mark I computer effort.

In 1950 he published the other of those two most influential papers, *Computing Machinery and Intelligence*, in Mind. In this article the Turing Test was described. In 1951 he was elected Fellow of the Royal Society. In the next few years he devoted much attention to the problem of morphogenesis in plants, including the writing of computer programs to pursue his studies. In 1954 he died under mysterious circumstances; it is mostly thought that he committed suicide due to society's lack of acceptance of a homosexual lifestyle, but accidental poisoning could not be ruled out.

Endnotes

---

[1] Hodges (1983).

[2] Despite the name, English Public schools are private. In Turing's day, it was essential to attend a Public school if one intended to go to Oxford or Cambridge.

[3] A typical Oxbridge Bachelor's degree takes three years, unlike the four normally undertaken in American universities.

2
Computability

Background

At the end of the nineteenth century, physicists believed that they were on the brink of an era when the all the remaining issues in physics were in the form of dotting the i's and crossing the t's of the then current understanding. There existed substantial and successful theories in the various fields of physics, such as dynamics (dealing with forces and movements), statics (dealing with stresses and strains, tensions and torsions), optics (dealing with properties of light), fluid dynamics (dealing with flows of liquids and gases), thermodynamics (dealing with heat and energy), and electromagnetics (dealing with electricity and magnetism), that seemed to be internally consistent and agreed substantially with experiment. It seemed that the remaining work was that of tying up a few loose ends and determining physical constants to a sufficient number of decimal places. There were some knotty problems, though. The constancy of the speed of light as embodied in the work of James Clerk Maxwell was inconsistent with the notion of relative velocity in Newtonian mechanics, which implied that by moving fast enough you could catch up with light. The reconciliation came from Albert Einstein in the form of his special theory of relativity. This in turn caused problems since Newtonian theory implied instantaneous transmission of gravitation, which special relativity forbade; Einstein came to the rescue again, this time with general relativity. At around the same time, Max Planck tackled a thorny problem in thermodynamics by suggesting that energy came in discrete units, or quanta; this gave rise to the highly successful theory of quantum mechanics. Together, relativity and quantum mechanics caused the field of theoretical physics to be turned on its head, and all the previously held theories of the very small and the very large to be thrown out.[1]

Mathematics too was in for some nasty surprises. One of these was provided by the great British philosopher and mathematician Bertrand Russell, the author with Alfred North Whitehead of the renowned *Principia Mathematica*. The German logician Frege had in 1884 introduced the idea of defining concepts in terms of sets; in particular, numbers. Thus the integer N was identified with the (infinite) collection of all sets with N elements. Logicians were therefore dealing now with not just sets but sets of sets, where all of the "inner" sets had a property in common. Russell considered the set S defined as

S is the set of all sets that are not members of themselves.

While this might look like frivolous word-play, it at the same time does appear to have a well-defined mathematical meaning. First we might ask how a set can be a member of itself. Consider the following set property: the set has two or more members. It is easy to come up with examples of sets with this property: the set of sexes, the set of continents, the set of colours, the set of integers. Let R be the set of all sets with this property. R clearly has more than two members, so is a member of itself. But what about Russell's set S? Is S a member of itself? If it is, then it obeys the set property that it is not a member of itself. On the other hand, if it is not a member of itself, it passes S's set membership requirements, so is duly a member of itself. This paradox caused a great deal of difficulty in the world of mathematical logic. It was clearly necessary that paradoxes and contradictions be absent from reasoning. From the time of Euclid the mathematical method was to start with a collection of accepted truths, known as axioms, and procedures for generating derivative truths by trusted methods known as rules of inference. It was necessary that only truths be derivable by such methods, and so some tightening up of these logical methods was necessary to avoid running into trouble. The formalized system that Russell and Whitehead produced was described in their aforementioned *Principia*. Meanwhile, the German mathematician David Hilbert took a different approach, but before we look at that, a few more words should be said about Russell's paradox.

An essential ingredient of the paradox is that it employed the method, or trick, if you like, of applying a property to itself. This method seems to appear around every corner in the passages of mathematical logic, and will show up a couple more times in this book. These methods use a technique sometimes known as *diagonalization*, after the proof by the 19th century German mathematician Georg Cantor that the real numbers are not the same as the rationals. Because of the importance of the diagonalization method to much of the material in this book, Cantor's proof is given here.

Any set is *enumerable* (or countable) by definition if its members can be put in 1-1 correspondence with the integers (or a subset of them). Consider the rational numbers in the range 0-1. Every such number can be expressed as the ratio of two integers n/d. List the rationals in the following order. First the (single) rational 0/1 where the numerator and denominator sum to 1. Then the (single) rational 0/2 where the numerator and denominator sum to 2. Then, in increasing order of numerator, those where the sum is 3: 0/3 and 1/2. Then those where the sum is 4: 0/4, 1/3. Then 5: 0/5, 1/4, 2/3. And so on. By reference to Figure 1, it is easily seen that we are merely following along diagonal stripes from lower-left to upper-right, where the stripes themselves move rightwards.

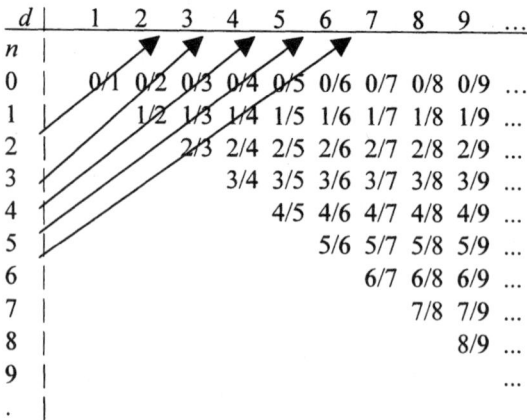

Figure 1.

Clearly every rational has a fixed position in this list and hence can be mapped to an integer. And we haven't even worried about reducing to lowest terms and eliminating duplicates, so we have overcounted and still been in good shape. What Cantor did, though,

6

was to show that this could not be done for the real numbers. His proof is an example of *reductio ad absurdum* – the method which makes an initial supposition, then shows that some clearly impossible consequence follows necessarily by means of a series of indisputable logical steps. The inevitable conclusion is that the initial hypothesis is false.

Suppose that the real numbers could be counted. Then they could be laid out in turn, something like this:

1st real: 0.9823459604904540546464234...   (say)
2nd real: 0.24875927520752308532085...   (say)
3rd real: 0.79823459327592720937409...   (say)
...

Now construct a real number Z between 0 and 1 as follows. Start with a decimal point. Then add any digit that is different from the first decimal digit of the first real (i.e. different from 9, in our example, shown in bold). Now append any digit different from the second digit of the second real (i.e. different from 4). Now append any digit different from 8, and so on. The real number so created will be different from any on the list, thus contradicting the assumption that the list was complete. Thus the reals cannot be placed in one-to-one correspondence with the natural numbers; in other words the reals cannot be counted.

The great German mathematician David Hilbert, arguably the best mathematician of his time, made several contributions of considerable importance. For example, he introduced the concept of a certain infinite-dimensional vector space – to be known as a Hilbert space – that would be an essential component of the theory of quantum mechanics. In Paris in 1900, at the International Mathematical Congress, he listed a number of important unsolved problems as challenges to the mathematicians of the new century. To this day, a number of these remain unsolved. One of these original problems, reflecting what might be described as a typical Teutonic desire for orderliness, was the question of whether there existed an algorithmic procedure for settling, in essence, any mathematical problem. This problem, known as the *Entscheidungsproblem* (Decision Problem), was one that Hilbert believed would have a positive answer. Turing, as we shall see, proved the case to be otherwise.

One of the difficulties posed for mathematicians at the time was what precisely was a mechanical procedure. These were the days before computers, so there were no such machines from whose principles of operation any such intuition could be developed. What Turing did was to create a formalism through which mechanical procedures could be described and analysed. Since (at the time) the only entities capable of carrying out procedures such as mathematical proofs were humans, Turing's concept of a machine included the brain. Thus the formalism he developed could be thought of simulating either the operation of a real mechanical device or a human brain.

Before we examine the brilliant creation of Turing, we shall look at how the first nails in the coffin of Hilbert's programme were hammered in. There were three related questions that concerned the foundations of mathematics, identified by Hilbert in 1928. 1. Whether mathematics was *consistent*, namely that if an assertion was provable, then its opposite was not. 2. Whether mathematics was *complete*, namely that every true statement was provable. 3. Whether mathematics was *decidable*, namely that there was an algorithm that could determine whether any given statement was true or not. In 1931, the Czech mathematician Kurt Gödel dealt this programme a crushing blow, by showing that any formal system such as arithmetic, if it is consistent then it cannot be complete. He achieved this by constructing an assertion that said, in effect, "this statement is not provable". His method, using a diagonalization technique, was as follows.[2] Gödel constructed a way of associating with any mathematical statement a unique natural number – this method is now known as *Gödel numbering*. Then *inter alia* every statement of the form

"The statement with Gödel number N cannot be proved."

will have some Gödel number. By suitable manipulation, Gödel constructed the statement S:

"The statement with Gödel number N_S cannot be proved."

with Gödel number N_S. S is not provable within the system in which it was constructed; this is what S says "inside," so S must be true.

Recall that in any consistent system, the negation of a true statement cannot be proven. Therefore neither S nor its negation are provable; this makes S undecidable and the system is incomplete.[3]

The Turing Machine

It was up to Alan Turing to prove that mathematics was not

decidable, and this was also done by diagonalization, as we shall see shortly. In the course of his demonstration, though, he defined and described a kind of machine which has come to embody for mathematicians and computer scientists the very notion of computability. This machine has come to be known as the *Turing machine*.

In developing his machine, Turing had to wrestle with questions of infinity, namely which aspects of the machine had to be finite and which could be infinite. A machine which executes a procedure has to have a number of internal states. It is clear that the number of these states must be finite, although it could be large. This does not limit the machine's ability to perform calculations of arbitrary size, since these states could be visited and revisited a large number of times. The procedure embodied in these states would have to operate for inputs of unknown size and to produce outputs of unknown size. Therefore the input/output medium (Turing chose a paper tape[4]) would have to be infinite (or at least there would have to be some means by which it could grow to accommodate whatever information was needed to be placed there).

There would have to be some language by which information was conveyed to the machine as input and to the outside world as output. This would be in the form of an alphabet of symbols, written on the tape. Turing makes the point that the alphabet has to be finite, or else if there were an infinite number of them there would be problems in telling some of them apart. Finally, the machine would embody a set of rules, which would direct how the machine operated. These rules would have to be finite in number.

Let us see how Turing describes the machine himself.

> Computing is normally done by writing certain symbols on paper. We may suppose this paper is divided into squares like a child's arithmetic book. In elementary arithmetic the two-dimensional character of the paper is sometimes used. But such a use is always avoidable, and I think that it will be agreed that the two-dimensional character of paper is no essential of computation. I assume then that the computation is carried out on one-dimensional paper, i.e., on a tape divided into squares. I shall also suppose that the number of symbols which may be printed is finite. If we were to allow an infinity of symbols, then there would be symbols differing to an

arbitrarily small extent[†]. The effect of this restriction of the number of symbols is not very serious. It is always possible to use sequences of symbols in the place of single symbols. Thus an Arabic numeral such as 17 or 9999999999999999 is normally treated as a single symbol. Similarly in any European language words are treated as single symbols (Chinese, however, attempts to have an enumerable infinity of symbols). The differences from our point of view between the single and compound symbols is that the compound symbols, if they are too lengthy, cannot be observed at one glance. This is in accordance with experience. We cannot tell at a glance whether 9999999999999999 and 999999999999999 are the same.

The behavior of the computer at any moment is determined by the symbols which he is observing, and his state of mind at that moment. We may suppose that there is a bound B to the number of symbols or squares which the computer can observe at one moment. If he wishes to observe more, he must use successive observations. We will also suppose that the number of states of mind which need be taken into account is finite. The reasons for this are of the same character as those which restrict the number of symbols. If we admitted an infinity of states of mind, some of them will be arbitrarily close and will be confused. Again this restriction is not one which seriously affects computation, since the use of more complicated states of mind can be avoided by writing more symbols on the tape. Let us imagine the operations performed by the computer to be split up into simple operations which are so elementary that it is not easy to imagine them further divided. Every such operation consists of some change of the

---

[†] If we regard a symbol as literally printed on a square we may suppose that the square is $0 < x < 1, 0 < y < 1$. The symbol is defined as a set of points in this square, viz. the set occupied by printers ink. If these sets are restricted to be measurable, we can define the distance between two symbols as the cost of transforming one symbol into the other if the cost of moving a unit area of printers ink unit distance is unity, and there is an infinite supply of ink at $x = 2, y = 0$. With this topology the symbols form a conditionally compact space [Turing's note].

physical system consisting of the computer and his tape. We know the state of the system if we know the sequence of symbols on the tape, which of these are observed by the computer (possible with a special order), and the state of mind of the computer. We may suppose that in a simple operation not more than one symbol is altered. Any other changes can be split up into simple changes of this kind. The situation in regard to the squares whose symbols may be altered in this way is the same as in regard to the observed squares. We may, therefore, without loss of generality, assume that the squares whose symbols are changed are always observed squares.

Besides these changes of symbols, the simple operations must include changes of distribution of observed squares. The new observed squares must be immediately recognisable by the computer. I think it is reasonable to suppose that they can only be squares whose distance from the closest of the immediately previously observed squares does not exceed a certain fixed amount. Let us say that each of the new observed squares is within L squares of an immediately previously observed square.

In connection with immediate recognisability, it may be thought that there are other kinds of squares which are immediately recognisable. In particular, squares marked by special symbols might be taken as immediately recognisable. Now if these squares are marked only by single symbols there can be only a finite number of them, and we should not upset our theory by adjoining these marked squares to the observed squares. If, on the other hand, they are marked by a sequence of symbols, we cannot regard the process of recognition as a simple process. This is a fundamental point and should be illustrated. In most mathematical papers the equations and theorems are numbered. Normally the numbers do not go beyond (say) 1000. It is, therefore, possible to recognise a theorem at a glance by its number. But if the paper was very long, we might reach Theorem 1577677334377; then further on in the paper, we might find ...hence (applying Theorem 1577677334377) we have .... In order to make sure which was the relevant theorem we should have to compare the two numbers figure by figure, possible ticking the figures off in pencil to make sure of their not being counted twice. If in spite of this it is still thought that there are other immediately recognisable squares, it does not upset my contention as long as these squares can be found by some process of which my tape machine is capable.

The simple operations must therefore include:

(a) Changes of the symbol on one of the observed squares.

(b) Changes of one of the squares observed to another square within L squares of one of the previously observed squares.

It may be that some of these changes necessarily involve a change of state of mind. The most general single operation must therefore be taken to be one of the following:

(A) A possible change (a) of symbol together with a possible change of state of mind.

(B) A possible change (b) of observed squares, together with a possible change of state of mind.

The operation actually performed is determined, as has been suggested (above) by the state of mind of the computer and the observed symbols. In particular, they determine the state of mind of the computer after the operation.

We may now construct a machine to do the work of this computer. To each state of mind of the computer corresponds an m -configuration of the machine. The machine scans B squares corresponding to the B squares observed by the computer. In any move the machine can change a symbol on a scanned square or can change any one of the scanned squares to another square distant not more than L squares from one of the other scanned squares. The move which is done, and the succeeding configuration, are determined by the scanned symbol and the m -configuration. The machines just described do not differ very essentially from computing machines as defined (previously) and corresponding to any machine of this type a computing machine can be constructed to compute the same sequence, that is to say the sequence computed by the computer.

Formulations of the Turing Machine

In discussing machines such as the Turing machine it is frequently necessary to consider the equivalence of two different machines. Two machines M_A and M_B are *equivalent* if for every possible input they compute the same output.[5] This says nothing about the number of internal states (what Turing calls 'state of mind'), the number or kind of state-change operations the machine can undergo, or how many steps it will take either machine for a given problem.

While Turing considers the possibility that a machine can scan B (>1) squares of tape at a time, it can be shown that for any such machine an equivalent machine can be constructed that scans a single square at a time. Such a formulation is the one traditionally given for Turing machines.

A Turing machine can be defined as follows. It is a finite-state machine which is free to move along a doubly infinite tape divided into squares on which symbols may be printed. These symbols are from an alphabet A, which includes "blank". The machine has a set S of possible states. At any given time t it is in one of the states of S – let us call this $s(t)$[6] – and is scanning a square of its tape on which is printed a symbol from A – let us call this $a(t)$ – this is the machine's input at t. Its response to the input (which is therefore a function both of the input and its current state) is trifold: it may change its state, it may write a new symbol on the tape – its output – and it may move one square to the left or right. Thus $s(t+1) = F(s(t), a(t))$; $a(t+1) = G(s(t), a(t))$; $d(t+1) = H(s(t), a(t))$, where d is the direction of movement, for some functions F, G and H. Equivalently, a Turing machine can be defined simply by a set of quintuples $\{(s_i, a_j, s_{ij}, a_{ij}, d_{ij})$,[7] that is, a set of objects with five "slots":

$$\begin{pmatrix} s_i & = & the\,current\,state \\ a_j & = & the\,symbol\,scanned \\ s_{ij} & = & the\,new\,state \\ a_{ij} & = & the\,symbol\,written \\ d_{ij} & = & the\,direction\,of\,movement \end{pmatrix}$$

It is a striking characteristic of the Turing machine how parsimonious Turing was of components for it, but it is utterly characteristic of pure mathematicians in general, and Turing in particular. Often what makes mathematical proofs elegant or even beautiful is the way the problem is stripped away to its bare essentials. As an example of this think back to the demonstration earlier that the reals were uncountable. To make the proof it is merely sufficient to show that the reals in any interval are uncountable – the traditional proof uses the interval 0-1. It might be more dramatic to consider the interval 0-.000000001 or something even tinier; after all, if the reals in such a small interval are uncountable then *surely* the reals in totality are, but such antics are logically unnecessary and are eschewed by mathematicians.[8] Turing's own preferences were clear from his writings when only 13 years old regarding his beloved chemistry experiments:[9]

> I always seem to want to make things from the thing that is commonest in nature and with the least waste in energy.

There are many alternative formulations of the Turing machine, all equivalent to the one given above, but which are more convenient for one particular proof or demonstration or another. These include: machines with a tape that is only infinite in one direction, machines with multiple tapes, machines with an alphabet of just two symbols,[10] machines with just two states,[11] or machines with a small value for the product of states and symbols.[12] As an illustration of a simple Turing machine, consider the following set of 6 quintuplets which define a machine which determines the parity of a binary number. The machine has states "0" and "1" (and "Halt") and it starts in "0". It is assumed that the machine is positioned on the left-most "1", and that the number is terminated at the right end with an "A". The machine will move to the right until it encounters the A, erasing any "1"s along the way. It will replace the "A" with a "1" or a "0" depending on the computed parity, and halt. Recall that the components of the quintuple are, in turn: current state, current input, new state, output, direction moved.

(0, 0, 0, 0, R)
(0, 1, 1, 0, R)
(0, A, Halt, 0, -)
(1, 0, 1, 0, R)
(1, 1, 0, 0, R)
(1, A, Halt, 1, -)

The machine starts as shown in Figure 2:

14

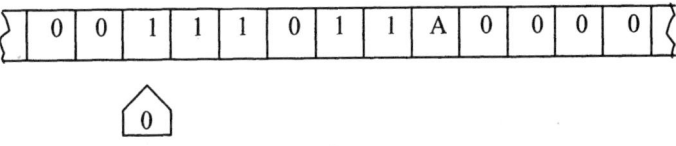

Figure 2.

And ends as shown in Figure 3:

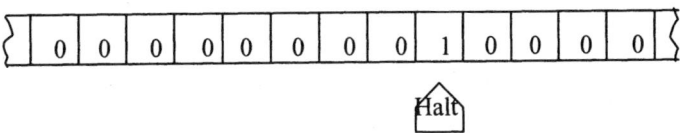

Figure 3.

Simple though it is, it is important to recognize that the machine computes a function. The particular function is the parity function, and in the example given it computes the parity of the binary number 111011 (decimal 59) to be 1. One might reasonably ask two questions: "Does every Turing machine compute a function?" and "Is there a Turing machine for every function?". We will address these questions in subsequent sections.

The Church-Turing Thesis

We all have informal notions of what a procedure is – a cooking recipe is a good example – but can the concept be formalized sufficiently for use in mathematical proofs? This question lies behind the notion of a *effective procedure*, that is, an algorithm which by following we can be guaranteed we find the correct solution to a problem. The important issue here is not whether the procedure has been formulated correctly – an algorithm to square a number simply by multiplying it by 2 is incorrect (except for the input of 2), but is still effective – but whether choosing what the next step is and how to carry it out is well-determined.

We can say, as does Minsky,[13] that an effective procedure tells us (or a machine) precisely how to behave, but there remains the problem that different people may disagree over the interpretation of a given rule. If, however, the entity doing the interpretation is a machine as simple as a Turing machine, then there is no room for such ambiguity.

Can a single machine carry out all effective procedures? Turing machines can carry out simple arithmetic operations, but what about sophisticated computations, like the Flight Simulator program popular on PCs today? This might appear unlikely. To make matters more formal, we need a way of describing the set of behavioural rules in a manner that can be read in by a machine, and we need a machine which can read in these rules and carry them out precisely. These needs will be realized in the form of a universal Turing machine, described in the next section.

Although the parity machine described earlier is incredibly simple, Turing discovered that he could design machines to perform quite complex computations. The trick is in trading off the complexity of the problem with time and space – the unlimited nature of the Turing machine tape, and the need for even quite simple programs to take a huge number of steps to complete. So can Turing machines be used for every effective procedure? It is not possible to prove this explicitly. Were one to be able to demonstrate that a particular effective procedure was not computable on a Turing machine, then this would be a proof (of the negative case), but none has been found.

At the same time that Turing was working with these machines, the American Alonzo Church, along with Stephen Kleene, was developing his theory of the *lambda-calculus*. This did not involve the same kind of mechanical devices, but was a more abstract mathematical/logical approach to Hilbert's *Entscheidungsproblem*. Church used abstraction to implement function definition. His notation employed a *dummy variable*, denoted by a preceding lambda, which identified 'slots' in the expression to the immediate right; these slots were to be filled by whatever followed the entire lambda-expression. Thus $\lambda x.[f(x)]$ would be a lambda-expression; when applied to an argument a, say, would equal $\lambda x.[f(x)]a = f(a)$, so the expression is equivalent to the function f.[14] The lambda-expressions are functions which, when applied to functions, produce other functions. Thus $\lambda fx.[f(f(x))]$ when applied to any function g produces $\lambda x.[g(g(x))]$; this latter function when applied to any argument y produces $g(g(y))$. Therefore $\lambda fx.[f(f(x))]$ produces the double application of its argument (in our example the function g); Church identifies this with the natural number 2. Similarly, $\lambda fx.[f(f(f(x)))]$ is identified with 3 and likewise for all positive integers; 0 is $\lambda fx.[x]$. Arithmetic operations on these functional equivalents of numbers are possible too. Addition is defined by $\lambda fgxy.[((fx)(gx))y]$, multiplication by $\lambda fgx.[f(gx)]$, exponentiation by $\lambda fg.[fg]$. Other functions can be built out of these. Ultimately, Church was able to show that every algorithmic operation could be represented by a lambda expression.

Turing believed that any process which could naturally be called an effective procedure could be realized by a Turing machine. He and Church were able to show the equivalence of their respective formalisms – any function representable as a lambda-expression could be implemented as a Turing machine, and vice-versa. This somewhat surprising result allowed the assertion that the notion of computability was a valid abstract mathematical notion, not tied to any particular mechanism or language. This was later reinforced by the demonstration that other formulations of effectiveness, such as Emil Post's canonical systems[15] and Kleene's general recursive functions,[16] were all equivalent. The proposition that any process that can naturally be called an effective procedure can be realized by a Turing machine (or any of its equivalents) is variously known as Turing's Thesis, Church's Thesis or the Church-Turing Thesis.

The Universal Turing Machine

Consider the Turing machine defined by the quintuples of Figure 4:

(0, x, 1, x, R)   x stands for any symbol
(1, x, 0, x, L)

Figure 4.

Suppose the machine starts in state "0". Then whatever the symbol it is reading, it moves to the right and changes to state "1". Then, whatever symbol is written there, it moves to the left and reverts to state "0". It is now in exactly the same situation as it started in, and so it loops forever. The same thing happens if it starts in state "1". A machine that does not halt does not compute a function in any reasonable sense. One can easily design a machine that halts for some inputs, but not for others. One might ask whether it is possible to tell algorithmically whether a given machine halts for a given input tape. That is, is there an effective procedure for deciding this? If there is, then it can be realized by a Turing machine. So the question becomes, can we build a Turing machine which will tell whether a machine will halt on a given input tape? The answer, it will turn out, is No.

The problem was raised earlier of whether a single machine could be defined which would tell whether a procedure was effective. Due to the results of the previous section, we know that this is equivalent to asking whether a universal Turing machine U can be built which will tell us how another machine T would behave for a given input. Concretely, since the only input to a Turing machine is a tape with symbols written on it, we need to find a way to represent T as a sequence of symbols. This is fortunately straightforward to do.

It was mentioned earlier that there are many equivalent formulations of a Turing machine. Therefore we will assume without loss of generality that the machine T to be represented has a semi-infinite tape and is a two-symbol machine. The input tape to U consists of a complete description of T at any stage in its computation. The format is as follows. From an identified point P on U's tape stretching to the left for as far as necessary is T's input tape. At some point within this segment is a marker M representing T's reading head. To the right of P are written, in order, the current state of T, the current symbol under T's reading head, then the quintuples of T (see Figure 5). A marker such as X is used for punctuation. The tape to the right of the last quintuple is used as U's working storage. Since U is fixed and T is arbitrary, T's alphabet may easily exceed U's, so we represent T's states as binary numbers, which require only two symbols (plus one as a delimiter).

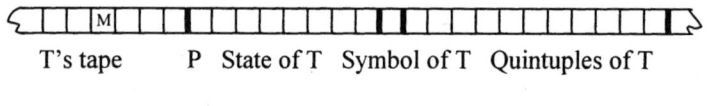

T's tape   P   State of T   Symbol of T   Quintuples of T

Figure 5.

The complete description of U will not be given here (the reader is referred to Minsky (1972) for details). The high-level operation can be described as quite similar to the way a human would check the operation of a machine – such as the parity checker described earlier. U will find the quintuple that corresponds to T's current state and symbol, and look up the new symbol, new state and direction. The new state will be written in the segment allocated for it, the new symbol will be written at the location of the marker M, M will be moved to the left or right as appropriate, and the symbol it over-writes will be transferred to the segment allocated for current symbol.

The machine just described will simulate[17] the operation of any Turing machine with any input tape. It might be worthwhile to dwell for a moment on the difference between T on the one hand, and U given T's description as input on the other. They both compute the same result, but there is an essential difference. When T operates it does not get to "see" its quintuples or to "introspect" in any way on its operation. In the terminology of computer programming language theory, T's instructions are *compiled* while U's are *interpreted*. Running a compiled program is always much faster than running an interpreter, but interpretation has the advantage that it admits much more readily such meta-operations of tracing, monitoring, logging and so on. For example, if we wish to know how many times T enters a given state while operating, we have to make changes to T's actual definition if we are to do this to T itself, but it is a simple matter to adapt U to monitor and record such state transitions (of T, not U!).

There is a tantalizing correspondence between the computer operations of interpretation and compilation, and the human conditions of what we will call *cognitive* and *sub-cognitive* thought. During cognitive thought, such as following explicitly instructions such as in a recipe, or following printed directions to an unfamiliar destination, we are consciously aware of the specific steps we are taking, and can easily recite what we are doing to an observer, or explain what we have done afterwards. Sub-cognitive thought usually occurs after we have practiced a procedure sufficiently that it becomes "second nature" to us. While this give us more facility at the task, it is usually associated with much greater difficulty to either change it or to explain it to others. There is often little to distinguish sub-cognitive thought from simple recall. If we are asked to multiply 23 by 32 we follow the procedure of long multiplication we are taught in school and can easily relate these steps to others. If asked to multiply 2 by 3 we answer "6" immediately but might have a little difficulty "proving" the answer. In the early days of learning a language, when faced with a problem of translation to the new language we laboriously translate each word in turn, struggling with the appropriate conjugations, declensions and word-order. When we have learned the language we can translate almost instantaneously, but maybe have to pause a bit if asked to justify the translation.

The computer programming language LISP,[18] invented by logician and artificial-intelligence pioneer John McCarthy in the 1950's, is built around Church's lambda-calculus. LISP, and languages based on it, was the primary language for writing AI programs in the 1960's and 70's, and is still used today, but primarily in academia. Prolog,[19] invented by Alain Colmerauer around 1970, is the other base language for AI. Prolog is based on Horn-clause[20] representation of first-order predicate calculus. In both of these languages, language statements are easily treated as data items for inspection, modification

19

and creation by the program itself. While most languages used to build commercial applications are compiled, LISP and Prolog are generally interpreted.

The Halting Problem – Part I

We asked earlier if it was possible to construct a Turing machine D which, if presented with the description of another Turing machine T and its tape, would tell us if T would halt on that tape. We asserted that it was not possible, and in this section we demonstrate it. This is such an important result that we present two entirely different looking proofs, although they are at their core intimately related. Both proofs use the technique of *reductio ad absurdum*.

First, we assume that D exists. We will denote the description of a Turing machine T as d_T, and its tape as t. We note from Figure 5 that the input to a universal Turing machine consists of a machine's tape followed by the machine's description. We represent this tape sequence symbolically as (t, d_T). Now, we are supposing that D can solve the halting problem for (t, d_T), for any T and any t. Nothing stops us using d_T as a particular value for t. So D solves the halting problem for (d_T, d_T). We'll use the convention of $D(d_T, d_T)$ to represent the application of machine D to tape (d_T, d_T). We can easily construct a machine E which replicates its input and then passes control to D. So $E(d_T) = D(d_T, d_T)$ will solve the halting problem.

What does "solve the halting problem" mean in case of $E(d_T)$? It means it must print 0 and halt if T does not halt, print 1 and halt if T does halt. Without loss of generality we can suppose it contains pre-halt states G_N and G_Y which are the sole precursors to halting. Then there will be quintuples in E's description which look like those in Figure 6:

$(G_N, x, Halt, 0, -)$ x stands for any symbol
$(G_Y, x, Halt, 1, -)$

Figure 6.

We now construct a new machine E* by adding two new states N_L and N_R to E and changing the two quintuples in Figure 6 to the four in Figure 7.

$(G_N, x, Halt, 0, -)$ x stands for any symbol
$(G_Y, x, N_R, 1, R)$

20

(N_R, x, N_L, x, L)
(N_L, x, N_R, x, R)

Figure 7.

Note that the third and fourth quintuples in Figure 7 are the looping pair from Figure 4; the second one is the second one in Figure 6 modified to enter the loop instead of halting. So $E^*(d_T)$ has the property that if T does not halt on d_T, E^* halts, and if T halts on d_T, E^* does not halt.

To complete the proof, we consider $E^*(d_{E^*})$; we simply substitute "E^*" for T in the last sentence of the previous paragraph and get: $E^*(d_{E^*})$ has the property that if E^* does not halt on d_{E^*}, E^* halts, and if E^* halts on d_{E^*}, E^* does not halt. This is clearly a contradiction, which means that none of E^*, E or D can exist.

The Halting Problem – Part II

The set of quintuples of a Turing machine, represented in binary and concatenated as in Figure 5, form a binary number. This can be viewed as the index number of the Turing machine, so that if the description of machine T is number n, then T is the nth Turing machine, or T_n. We will ignore in this presentation the somewhat messy details of delimiters and coding – the interested reader is referred to Penrose (1989). We will assume for now that the input tape is in binary, so it too can be represented by an integer.

With this mapping, each Turing machine has a number, and each natural number corresponds to a Turing machine, although in most cases to severely dysfunctional ones. A large number of these machines will not halt for some or all inputs. We can draw a table where the nth row corresponds to the machine T_n, the mth column corresponds to the input tape's number m, the cell to the result of the computation (see Figure 8). The "∞" indicates the machine does not halt on that input. The entries are just for illustrative purposes and may or may not correspond to the actual behaviour of the machine.

21

m	0	1	2	3	4	5	6	7	8	9 ...
n										
0	∞	∞	∞	∞	∞	∞	∞	∞	∞	∞ .
1	1	1	1	1	1	1	1	1	1	1 .
2	0	0	0	0	0	0	0	0	0	0 .
3	0	1	∞	∞	∞	∞	∞	∞	∞	∞ .
4	∞	0	0	0	0	0	0	0	0	0 .
5	∞	0	∞	0	∞	0	∞	0	∞	0 .
6	0	1	2	3	4	5	6	7	8	9 .
7	0	∞	0	1	∞	0	1	2	∞	3 .
8	0	1	4	9	16	25	36	49	64	81 .
.	.	.	.	.	.	.	.	.	.	.
.	.	.	.	.	.	.	.	.	.	.

Figure 8.

In Figure 8, the value of cell (m, n) is $C(m)$. To actually calculate this table for real would require calculating the output of every Turing machine for every input. This would be problematic for the cases where the machine does not halt. Recall machine D, which by hypothesis produces a 0 if the machine-tape description on its input doesn't halt, and 1 if it does. $D(m, T_n)$ is zero in just those cases where $T_n = \infty$, and one otherwise. We can then recalculate every cell in Figure 7 by the following formula:

$$\text{Cell } (m, n) \text{ is } \begin{cases} T_n(m) & \text{if } D(m, T_n) = 1 \\ 0 & \text{otherwise} \end{cases}$$

This gives the table in Figure 9.

22

m	0	1	2	3	4	5	6	7	8	9 ...
n										
0	0	0	0	0	0	0	0	0	0	0 .
1	1	1	1	1	1	1	1	1	1	1 .
2	0	0	0	0	0	0	0	0	0	0 .
3	0	1	0	0	0	0	0	0	0	0 .
4	0	0	0	0	0	0	0	0	0	0 .
5	0	0	0	0	0	0	0	0	0	0 .
6	0	1	2	3	4	5	6	7	8	9 .
7	0	0	0	1	0	0	1	2	0	3 .
8	0	1	4	9	16	25	36	49	64	81 .
.	.	.	.	.	.	.	.	.	.	.
.	.	.	.	.	.	.	.	.	.	.

Figure 9.

The tables in Figures 8 and 9 both have the property that every computable sequence of numbers must occur in at least one row. The rows of Figure 9, though, have the additional property of being effectively computable, through the formula given above. Let us modify this formula for just those entries on the diagonal, by adding one, producing the table in Figure 10.

$$\text{Cell } (m, n) \text{ is} \begin{cases} if m=n & \begin{cases} T_n(m)+1 & if D(m,T_n)=1 \\ 1 & otherwise \end{cases} \\ if m \neq n & \begin{cases} T_n(m) & if D(m,T_n)=1 \\ 0 & otherwise \end{cases} \end{cases}$$

m	0	1	2	3	4	5	6	7	8	9 ...
n										
0	1	0	0	0	0	0	0	0	0	0 .
1	1	2	1	1	1	1	1	1	1	1 .
2	0	0	1	0	0	0	0	0	0	0 .
3	0	1	0	1	0	0	0	0	0	0 .
4	0	0	0	0	1	0	0	0	0	0 .
5	0	0	0	0	0	1	0	0	0	0 .
6	0	1	2	3	4	5	7	7	8	9 .
7	0	0	0	1	0	0	1	3	0	3 .
8	0	1	4	9	16	25	36	49	65	81 .
.	.	.	.	.	.	.	.	.	.	.
.	.	.	.	.	.	.	.	.	.	.

Figure 10.

We therefore have in the diagonal the eminently computable sequence whose nth element is

$$\begin{cases} T_n(n)+1 & \text{if } D(n,T_n)=1 \\ 1 & \text{otherwise} \end{cases}$$

However, by its construction, this sequence differs from every row, hence from every computable sequence. Hence we have a contradiction.

This second proof of the insolvability of the halting problem was another use of diagonalization. The first proof avoided the need to enumerate all the Turing machines, but both employed the device of applying a machine to its own description. In any case, Hilbert's *Entscheidungsproblem* is demonstrated to be unsolvable.

Non-Computable Functions

One of the characteristics of the field of mathematical logic is that, to the layman at least, there are so many counter-intuitive results. This may be because a number of the terms of the art, words such as computable, countable, decidable, are everyday English words, although they take on precise meanings within this formalism. One such surprising result is that there exist functions that are not

24

computable.

If a function is computable, then there exists a Turing machine which, when given a description of the function and the argument (input) to the function, computes its output. Since every Turing machine's description is finite, it can be represented as a finite string in some alphabet. It is clear that, using techniques similar to those previously described, these Turing machines can be set up in 1-1 correspondence with the natural numbers, so the set of these Turing machines, i.e. the set of computable functions, is countably infinite. Let's just look at a subset of these functions,[21] namely those that map the integers to 0 and 1. These must be countable, so suppose they are set up in 1-1 correspondence with the natural numbers. Let f_i be the function corresponding to the ith integer. Consider the function:

$$F(n) = \begin{cases} 0 & \text{if } f_n(n) = 1 \\ 1 & \text{otherwise} \end{cases}$$

What integer does the function F correspond to? If it corresponds to j, then it must be f_j, by the definition of f_j. But by the definition of F, if $f_j(j) = 1$, then $F(j) = 0$, so $F \neq f_j$. This contradiction shows that F is not a computable function, another victim of diagonalization.

A Turing machine is an idealized computing device, and as has been discussed in this chapter, it can be used to demonstrate various theoretical facts about computability in general. None of today's computers looks like a Turing machine, although they are all equivalent to Turing machines (modulo the requirement for unlimited storage). For Turing, though, they served to crystallize the idea of a general-purpose computer. As he wrote about LCMS (Logical Computing Machines):[22]

> It is possible to describe LCMS in a very standard way, and to put the description into a form which can be 'understood' (i.e., applied by) a special machine. In particular it is possible to design a 'universal machine' which is an LCM such that if the standard description of some other LCM is imposed on the otherwise blank tape from outside and the (universal) machine then set going it will carry out the operations of the particular machine whose description it was given. ...

> The importance of the universal machine is clear. We do not need to have an infinity of different machines doing different

jobs. A single one will suffice. The engineering work of producing various machines for various jobs is replaced by the office work of 'programming' the universal machine to do these jobs.

Endnotes

---

[1] For a fascinating account of the search for the Theory of Everything, from relativity and quantum mechanics to string theory and beyond, see the excellent book by Brian Greene (1999).

[2] Gödel (1931).

[3] See the book on Gödel in this series by Jaakko Hintikka (2000).

[4] Even though Turing's construction was theoretical, it was clearly influenced by what was physically achievable. Magnetic storage such as we have in disk drives was not known at the time.

[5] Or neither one finishes its computation. This will be discussed in more detail later in the topic of the Halting Problem.

[6] Mathematicians understand a function to be a set of ordered pairs, but a less abstract definition is probably in order for the general reader. A function can be thought of as a repeatable and well-determined way of going from its inputs or *arguments* to its output or result. Usually a function is represented by a form like $f(x)$, which denotes the result of applying function f to argument x. Then if f is the function "multiply by 2 and add 3" we will have results like $f(1) = 5$ and $f(2) = 7$. Certain very common functions have special syntax; for example the *square* function is denoted by the superscript 2. Thus $3^2 = 9$ is just saying that the result of applying the *square* function to argument 3 is 9. Functions can have multiple arguments – for example the function *TriangleArea(x,y,z)* has three arguments, the lengths x , y and z of three sides of a triangle, and it returns the area of the triangle (when such a triangle exists). A very common function is addition, and as with the square function we have a special notation for it, namely the plus sign. This is just a syntactic issue – there is no difference between $x+y$ and *add(x,y)*.

In the particular instance of $s(t)$, s is the state function which when applied to a time t returns the state of the machine at that time. The functions F, G and H to be encountered shortly each take two arguments – the same two arguments to be precise – but compute different results.

[7] This notation, as well as some of the definitions and examples in this section, is adapted from Minsky (1972).

[8] Alan R. Baker, 1970 Fields medallist, in private conversations with the author.

[9] Hodges (1983) p. 19.

[10] See, for example, Penrose (1989).

[11] Shannon (1956).

[12] See, for example, Minsky (1972).

[13] Minsky (1972) p. 106.

[14] The development here is an abbreviated form of the discussion of Church's work in Penrose (1989).

[15] Post (1943).

[16] Kleene (1936). A *primitive-recursive* function is one which can be built from the zero function, the successor function, composition and primitive recursion – i.e. a base function plus an inductive step function. If a function can be built from primitive recursion along with minimalization (e.g. "the smallest x for which ...") then it is *general-recursive*.

[17] The word 'simulate' here does not carry with it any connotation of an approximation. The step-by-step details of the definition and operation of U are not the same as that of T, but the result left on the tape for a given input will be exactly the same.

[18] Officially, LISP stands for "LISt Processor", but is often believed to stand for "Lots of Irritating Superfluous Parentheses", because the syntax of the language uses parentheses heavily.

[19] Prolog stands for "Programmation en logique" (Programming in logic).

[20] Horn clauses are disjunctions of terms where at most one term is un-negated. Thus the English statement "All four-sided equilateral figures are squares", which is represented in Prolog by "square(X) :- four-sided(X), equilateral(X)." corresponds to the first-order logic expression "...X square(X) – ^four-sided(X) – ^equilateral(X)".

[21] Following Hopcroft and Ullman, Chapter 1.

[22] Turing (1948).

3

Codes and Computers

Usually when matters of life and death are discussed in the context of a philosopher (that is, if it is not a metaphysical discussion), it is generally about the untimely death of the philosopher himself – Socrates is a prime example. Alas, the same can also be said of Alan Turing, but only in part. Turing's work with cryptography caused, directly or indirectly, many deaths, but saved untold numbers more.

During World War II, he battled with a team of colleagues in rural England to decipher the communications of the German military. These communications were encrypted by means of a mechanical device known as the Enigma, and although Turing's team in Bletchley Park knew of the overall operation of the machine thanks to some early intelligence from the Poles,[1] the Germans were continually tweaking and improving the device. The team could, at times, decipher messages thanks to a combination of ingenuity, sheer hard work and some German sloppiness, but it stretched the team's resources enormously to do so. Coded messages would come in faster than the operation could decode them, and it was a huge challenge to get any message decoded quickly enough to be of use to the Allied authorities. When the Germans made changes to the machine, there would be bleak periods when nothing useful was forthcoming from Bletchley Park. The most desirable piece of additional equipment Turing and his co-workers could use was an actual – and recent – version of the Enigma machine itself. While obtaining such a device from German headquarters was out of the question, it was by the very nature of the encryption process used by the Enigma that the same machine was used for decryption.

Thus all German units in the field, including ships and submarines, carried an Enigma. When the British military realized this, and when they came to appreciate the importance of the intelligence coming out of Bletchley Park, they made capturing an Enigma a priority. This inevitably led to the deaths of more combatants[2] – at the time – but ultimately it helped greatly cut down on the shipping losses in the Atlantic and played a decidedly important role in bringing the War to a close.

The Enigma was an entirely mechanical device which translated individual letters into other letters. The basic machine employed a sequence of 3 rotors, each of which did letter-substitution. The machine was by design not reset between each letter encipherment, so that the letter with which an A, say, would get enciphered would depend on the current setting of the rotors, and hence the entire earlier part of the message. A particular property of the Enigma's method of operation is that the same machine could be used to decode messages, as long as the rotors on the decoding machine were initially set to the same positions as the rotors on the encoding machine. The method used to crack an Enigma code was to build a replica – Turing's device was called the Bombe – and attempt to discover the initial and internal rotor settings which gave rise to the message. The initial search space was large, but Turing's group did have some early successes, thanks in part to the intelligence information they got from the Poles. However, the Germans kept improving the device by means such as adding a plugboard in front, which gave rise to ever more combinations, and the German navy added a fourth rotor, making the task even more difficult. The decryption effort involved a combination of a process of elimination, thanks to clever tricks thought up by Turing to reduce the search space, hard work to test remaining alternatives, luck, and the occasional break from German carelessness or Allied intelligence. The period 1939-1942 at Bletchley was one of alternating successes and prolonged dry spells, but ultimately proved to be a major factor in turning the war around.[3]

Turing got involved with two other machines while at Bletchley Park. One, the Delilah, he designed and built himself. In early 1943 he had visited the Bell Laboratories in the U.S. and had immersed himself in learning about electronic speech encipherment. It was at Bell Labs that he met Claude Shannon, originator of Communication Theory, and profited from many conversations with him. Some time after Turing returned to England, he was able to devote time to work on projects other than the Enigma, and he turned to speech encipherment. The Delilah – what we would today call a scrambler – was not specifically important in its own right, except that it acted as a dress rehearsal for Turing's design of the ACE computer, which we will mention shortly. Ironically, during this latter part of the war period, there was another hardware design project ongoing – the Colossus – but Turing did not wish to be personally involved with the design of it. Hodges[4] suggests it was Turing's solitary nature that caused this behaviour. Several Colossi were completed, the first one in 1943. Although they were intended as special-purpose machines, they were entirely automatic and were extremely flexible.[5] Turing did involve himself with their programming and use, and could see from them directly the beneficial results of high-speed automatic computing devices.

The First Computer

There is no agreement among scientists (or historians of science for that matter) who was the inventor of the first computer, as we understand the word. Opinions seem to have as much to do with what side of the Atlantic the writer is on, as anything else!

Charles Babbage is often credited with inventing the computer, but he was by no means the first to have attempted to build a calculating device. We will not attempt here to catalogue all devices built since ancient times, but just list a few of the more historically significant ones; George Dyson's *Darwin among the Machines* would be an excellent resource for the interested reader. In the middle of the 17th century, the French mathematician Blaise Pascal, after whom the programming language PASCAL[6] is named, built an adding machine. This machine, along with the writings of materialist philosopher Thomas Hobbes, influenced the great German mathematician Gottfried Wilhelm von Leibniz, who invented his own calculating machine. This machine was based on decimal arithmetic, which we understand today is a poor choice for data representation in a general-purpose computer; however, Leibniz did identify the benefits of the binary system for both logic and computation, although it was centuries before any machine was built which used binary.[7]

There is no doubt Babbage 150 years later with his Analytical Engine (which he never completed) played an important role in the development of the computer, but his design was for an entirely mechanical machine. Electronics was unknown in the early nineteenth century, but Babbage was familiar with the use of electricity, including telegraphy, yet he declined to consider adopting its use for his Engine.[8] Babbage's design did include provisions for conditional program execution, but he had no notion of storing programs in the same form of data (which we nowadays consider to be the hallmark of a computer), and nor did he consider using the binary system (which is not theoretically required for a computer but has significant practical advantages).

There was much activity in both Europe and the United States at the time of the Second World War that ultimately led to the modern computer. Several separate important developments were made in different places at different times during this period.

In 1939, The Americans John Atanasoff and Clifford Berry designed (but never completed) the ABC, the first computer to use the binary system; this computer was electromechanical. The German Konrad Zuse built what could be described as the first automatically controlled calculator, the Z3, in 1941, used to help design military equipment. He invented the first programming language (the *Plankalkul*). He would likely have built the first general-purpose computer, but was unable to thanks to lack of government support.

In 1944, Howard Aiken of Harvard and engineers from IBM built the Mark I, another electromechanical device; this one was designed to produce accurate ordnance tables. In 1946, John Mauchly and J. Presper Eckert at the University of Pennsylvania after three years finished the ENIAC, generally regarded as the first fully electronic general-purpose computer. The ENIAC was a decimal machine, and only "stored" programs in the form of plug-boards attached to the main machine. The first real stored-program computer was the Mark I at the University of Manchester in 1948; the EDSAC at the University of Cambridge was completed and programmed by Maurice Wilkes, David Wheeler and others in 1949 and became the first machine to offer a regular computing service to a community of users.[9]

The reason that the ENIAC is usually accorded the honour of being the first general-purpose computer is that the Colossus, despite actually being a general-purpose computer, was designed and only used for the specific task of decryption – a fine distinction. Had war-time secrecy not prevailed in 1943, and had Turing had a more assertive and self-promoting personality, history might have been written differently.

If proposals rather than working prototypes can be considered contenders for priority, then there are two. In June 1945 John von Neumann published the EDVAC Report, in response to a government contract, and after extensive discussions with Mauchly and Eckert and others at U. Penn. The EDVAC (to be completed in 1950) was binary and stored programs internally in the form of mercury delay lines. A significant innovation was the *conditional goto* instruction (anticipated

31

by Babbage) which allowed program flow to be diverted based on the current state of the machine. The EDVAC report was widely distributed and was largely responsible for the term *von Neumann computer* becoming associated with the standard fetch-execute instruction cycle employed by almost all computers from then until today.

Just a few weeks after the EDVAC report came out, Alan Turing published the ACE report.[10] This document is a detailed proposal for an electronic computer; after much difficulty the proposal was funded and the Pilot Model was completed in 1950. This proposal was in no way based on the EDVAC report, but instead owed much to his work 10 years earlier on the universal Turing machine. As we saw in the previous chapter, instructions for Turing machines are encoded as numbers and treated as data by the universal Turing machine.

Turing's design philosophy was one of minimalism – the machine should have as few instruction types as possible. There was no provision even for a conditional branch instruction as in the EDVAC, but achieved the same functionality by over-writing of instructions in memory.[11] This mechanism relied on the equivalent treatment of program and data.

Perhaps the most important contribution to the field of programming from this report was the notion of a hierarchy of program segments – what we would today call subroutines.[12] The notion of a subroutine can be understood by anyone who cooks. A cooking recipe can be likened to a program, since it consists of a sequence of steps complete with loops and conditional branching. Sometimes a certain sequence of steps needs to be undertaken a number of times during the cooking process. Instead of these steps being written out in full every time they are called for (open the oven, insert toothpick into cake, withdraw it, examine it for adhesion), the sequence can be described once on the side and given the label "test-for-doneness". Then the step "test-for-doneness" can be included whenever needed, bracketed implicitly with the instructions "suspend what you are doing" and "resume what you were doing".

As we have mentioned before, and as was amply demonstrated by the elegant sparseness of the Turing machine formulation, Turing favoured simplicity in design. However, in the design of a real computer, there are many tradeoffs that have to be taken into consideration, including cost, ease of maintenance, size and speed. Even if these other criteria are fixed by external concerns, there remains a tradeoff that needs to be dealt with at the heart of the machine's design, and that is in the form of the instruction set. Just as a

Turing machine had instructions in the form of quintuples, so electronic computers have instructions, but the form is somewhat different.

One typical instruction type, and one that has been common in computers from the 1940's to today, is in the form of four segments: an operation code and three addresses (locations in memory), denoted perhaps as {OP, A, B, C}. For example, OP might correspond to ADD, the A and B being the addresses of the quantities to be added, and C being the address into which to store the result. This is not the only way to implement an add operation, though. Most computers have a special register in the arithmetic unit called the *accumulator*, which can be the implicit operand of a number of instructions. Thus the addition of two quantities can be implemented by the sequence of instructions:[13]

ZERO	zero the accumulator
ADD A	add A to the accumulator
ADD B	add B to the accumulator
STORE C	store the contents of the accumulator in C

Alternatively, the first two instructions in this sequence could be replaced by LOAD A – load the contents of A into the accumulator. It should be clear that the particular instructions available in a computer affect the way the software (the program) is written. Having a large variety of instruction types will allow for more compact coding, since it will happen more often that single instructions will be able to perform a logical operation. On the other hand, having a smaller number of more basic instructions leads to somewhat longer instruction sequences, but this is mitigated by the fact that these instructions can be executed more quickly. Turing favoured the latter approach,[14] and in so doing anticipated the interest that would follow decades later in RISC (Reduced Instruction Set Computers) machine architectures.

Turing realized from his knowledge of how mechanical hand-calculators were used to perform complex calculations that further economy could be achieved in programming by taking advantage of the repetitive nature of the intermediate steps. Just as a multiply instruction might be offered to the user as a single MULT op-code, but implemented in hardware by a series of additions, so more complicated functions could be enshrined in what Turing called a *subsidiary table*,[15] but is today known as a subroutine. A subroutine (recall "test-for-doneness") is a sequence of instructions with the special property that after being executed the control reverts to the place from which the subroutine was called. The subroutine can be called by many different places in the code, quite possibly with different arguments (inputs) each

Codes and Computers

time. Turing worked out the stack mechanism by which the return or link address could be saved for use at the end of the subroutine call. This was necessary since subroutines could call each other, giving rise to a dynamic hierarchy of calls, with time-varying stacks. In fact, a subroutine could even call itself. Take for example the factorial function. Mathematically, we can define:

$$n! = n.(n -1).(n-2).....3.2.1$$

A simple way to calculate $n!$ in a program is by iteration: to keep a running product (initialized to 1), and a running counter (also initialized to 1). The counter is incremented and the running total gets multiplied by the new counter, and the process repeats until the counter reaches n.[16] However, there exists an alternative mathematical definition:

$$n! = n . (n -1)! \quad (\text{and } 1! = 1)$$

Here $n!$ is defined in terms of $(n -1)!$. This suggests the following program, where we will use modern programming language syntax for clarity:

```
function FACTORIAL (integer N) {
   if (N = 1) then 1
   else N * FACTORIAL(N-1);
}
```

This is a recursive program, meaning that it refers to itself. Today we have both general-purpose programming languages and also specialized ones such as algebraic manipulation languages, logic programming languages and so on. For any of these to be useful to a computer there needs to be a program which takes programs written in such a language (the source) and either compiles it to a lower-level form or interprets it. Turing anticipated the advent of high-level languages:[17]

> I expect that digital computing machines will eventually stimulate a considerable interest in symbolic logic and mathematical philosophy. The language in which one communicates with these machines, i.e. the language of instruction tables, forms a sort of symbolic logic. The machine interprets whatever it is told in a quite definite

34

manner without any sense of humour or sense of proportion. Unless in communicating with it one says exactly what one means, trouble is bound to result. Actually, one could communicate with these machines in any language provided it was an exact language, i.e. in principle one should be able to communicate in any symbolic logic, provided that the machine were given instruction tables which would enable it to interpret that logical system. This would mean that there will be much more practical scope for logical systems than there has been in the past. Some attempts will probably be made to get the machine to do actual manipulations of mathematical formulae. To do so will require the development of a special logical system for the purpose. This system should resemble normal mathematical procedure closely, but at the same time should be as unambiguous as possible. As regards mathematical philosophy, since the machines will be doing more and more mathematics themselves, the center of gravity of the human interest will be driven further and further into philosophical questions of what can in principle be done etc.

Turing himself explored these philosophical questions in his paper *Computing Machinery and Intelligence*, which we discuss in the chapter after next. Before we do that, we will take a detour into the world of language, and investigate the relations between the study of language and Turing's work.

Endnotes

[1] Hodges (1983)

[2] The action-adventure movie *U-571* by United Artists (2000) is about the attempt to capture an Enigma from a German submarine.

[3] For a more detailed description of the code-breaking activity, see Hinsley and Stripp (1993) or Hodges (1983).

[4] Hodges (1983), p. 268.

[5] Randell (1973), pp. 296-297.

[6] The program snippets FACTORIAL and HANOI introduced on pages 43 and 78 respectively are written in a PASCAL-like syntax.

[7] Dyson (1997) pp. 36-37.

[8] Ibid. p.42.

[9] Lavington (1980).

[10] Turing (1945).

[11] Turing explains it thus:

> Suppose we wish to arrange that at a certain point instruction 33 will be applied if a certain digit is 0 but instruction 50 if it is 1. Then we may copy down these two instructions and then do a little calculation involving these two instructions and the digit D in question. One form the calculation can take is to pretend that the instructions were really numbers and calculate
>
> D x Instruction 50 + $(1-D)$ x Instruction 33.
>
> The result may then be stored away, let us say in a box which is permanently labelled 'Instruction 1'. We are then given an order ... saying that instruction 1 is to be followed, and the result is that we carry out instruction 33 or 50 according to the value of D.

[12] Turing describes the stack mechanism used to implement the nested calling of subroutines. This is the standard mechanism used today, except that the terms *push* and *pop* are used instead of *bury* and *unbury*:

> When we wish to start on a subsidiary operation we need only make a note of where we left off the major operation and then apply the first instruction of the subsidiary. When the subsidiary is over we look up the note and continue with the major operation. Each subsidiary operation can end with instructions for the recovery of the note. How is the burying and disinterring of the note to be done? There are of course many ways. One is to keep a list of these notes in one or more standard size delay lines (1024), with the most recent last. The position of the most recent of these will be kept in a fixed TS, and this reference will be modified every time a subsidiary is started or finished. The burying and disinterring processes are fairly elaborate, but there is fortunately no need to repeat the instructions involved each time, the burying being done through a standard instruction table BURY, and the disinterring by the table UNBURY.

(The TS referred to is a Temporary Storage unit, known better today as a *register*.)

[13] This program snippet is given in a typical *assembler* language., in

36

which for the most part instructions are direct symbolic representations of the binary machine code.

[14] Turing (1945) p. 3.

[15] Turing (1947) pp. 99-100.

[16] Or the counter could start at n and proceed downwards to 1. The result would be the same.

[17] Turing (1947).

4

Turing and Language

Perhaps unsurprisingly, Alan Turing did not pay much attention to the computational issues involved with language understanding, although his work sparked off an entire intellectual field of endeavor.[1] For centuries, the only groups who gave much thought to (or took advantage of) the semantic vagaries of language were politicians, lawyers and philosophers. In 1939, when Turing was a lecturer at Cambridge, he attended Ludwig Wittgenstein's course on Foundations of Mathematics. One of the debates between the two men concerned the Liar's Paradox (if someone says "I am lying," is he?).[2] Wittgenstein argued it is just a language game, and has no real consequence. Turing, ever the mathematician, could not accept such a glib analysis, since to a mathematician a single contradiction allows anything to be proven. Ironically, an alternative view was provided very publicly sixty years later by President William Clinton in his impeachment depositions: "It all depends on what the meaning of the word 'is' is." If 'is' bespeaks a general condition, but one which is not necessarily always true, and for which the speaker deliberately gives no indication of the current veracity, then the paradox disappears. However, treating words as semantic units whose meaning depends on the whim of the speaker (leaving aside issues of polysemy[3]) is the antithesis of any systematic behaviour of language required by attempts to process it by mechanical means.[4]

Mathematicians skirted such problems with language by inventing one of their own – the symbol system known as mathematics! –

wherein each of the tokens has a precise meaning. Mathematical problems may originate in the real world, but are represented as word problems (either explicitly or implicitly) which are then re-represented as mathematical expressions. The equations that then result are solved using the appropriate branches of theory. What was never given much thought was the process of converting from a linguistic representation, which carries all the ambiguity and imprecision of language, to a formal mathematical representation. Both Hilbert and Turing, as all mathematicians in fact, took as their respective starting points problems represented in mathematics, without seeming to consider whether the problem of generating the mathematical representation was of equivalent complexity as (or maybe more than) that of solving the mathematics itself. Indeed, Turing states in a paper on game-playing:[5]

> *If one can explain quite unambiguously in English, with the aid of mathematical symbols if required, how a calculation is to be done, then it is always possible to programme any digital computer to do that calculation, provided the storage capacity is adequate.* [Turing's italics]
>
> This is not the sort of thing that admits of a clear-cut proof, but amongst workers in the field is regarded as being clear as day.

While he did not explicitly consider the problem of converting problems expressed in English into a formalism suitable for direct processing on a computer, Turing was sensitive to the gulf that existed between the nature of a problem as it existed embedded in the real world, and its mechanical solution. The gulf had to be crossed with the aid of humans, and he clearly foresaw the advantages of mechanizing some of these processes. In the introduction to his proposal for the development of his ACE computer,[6] he states:

> Calculating machinery in the past has been designed to carry out accurately and moderately quickly small parts of calculations which frequently recur. The four processes addition, subtraction, multiplication and division, together perhaps with sorting and interpolation, cover all that could be done until quite recently, if we except machines of the nature of the differential analyzer and wind tunnels, etc. which operate by measurement rather than by calculation.

It is intended that the electronic calculator[7] now proposed should be different in that it will tackle whole problems. Instead of repeatedly using human labour for taking material out of the machine and putting it back at the appropriate moment all this will be looked after by the machine itself. This arrangement has very many advantages.

(1) The speed of the machine is no longer limited by the speed of the human operator.

(2) The human element of fallibility is eliminated, although it may to an extent be replaced by mechanical fallibility.

(3) Very much more complicated processes can be carried out than could easily be dealt with by human labour.

It is perhaps ironic that he was concerned with mechanical failure, only natural in the days when computers employed thousands of vacuum tubes, but did not consider the very human source of error in computing, that of writing software.

Computational Linguistics

Computational linguistics in Turing's time did not exist.[8] Despite the pioneering work of the German Jacob Grimm, the Swiss Frederick de Saussure and others, modern linguistics was exclusively a descriptive "science" even in the middle of the 20th century. The situation changed with the advent of the computer, since when it became plausible that a machine might be able to understand or generate language it became necessary to explain rather than just describe the multiple phenomena of language. The person to whom we can attribute responsibility for thus originating the discipline of Computational Linguistics was the American Noam Chomsky (who ironically was never much interested in the field himself, at least not in issues such as computational efficiency).

Formally, a language is described by a grammar. A grammar is a set of rules, called productions, by which certain combinations of the symbols of a given alphabet may be generated. Valid combination strings are called sentences; the set of all such sentences defines the language. The symbols in the alphabet are the terminal symbols of the grammar. There may also be what are called non-terminal symbols, whose function is somewhat like that of the internal states of a Turing machine. Let us look at the following very simple example of a grammar G; S is the start or sentence symbol; it along with A and B are non-terminal symbols; a and b are terminal symbols; ε is the empty string (see Figure 11). G generates the language L, which consists of all possible strings consisting of sequences of the pair 'ab' (ab, abab, ababab, abababab ...):[9]

$$S \to aB$$
$$B \to bA$$
$$A \to aB$$
$$A \to \varepsilon$$

Figure 11.

In addition to being able to generate languages, grammars can also be said to recognize them, by in effect running them in reverse. G can recognize any strings that consist of sequences of pairs of 'ab'. Strings such as 'a' or 'b' or 'aab' are not recognized (or generated) by G.

Chomsky defined four classes of grammars, which he called Type 0, 1, 2 and 3. Each Type was a proper superset of the next, in the sense that it could generate (or recognize) languages that the next Type could not. The simple grammar above is an example of a Type 3 or *regular* grammar; no regular grammar can generate all palindromes of a set of symbols (for example, the set of palindromes of the alphabet {a,b} includes a, b, aba, abba, ababa, babab, ...). This can be seen by understanding more of Chomsky's work.

Each of Chomsky's Types of grammar corresponds to a class of formal machine. Type 3 grammars correspond to what are called *finite-state machines* (FSMs) or *automata*. An FSM that corresponds to G is shown in Figure 12.

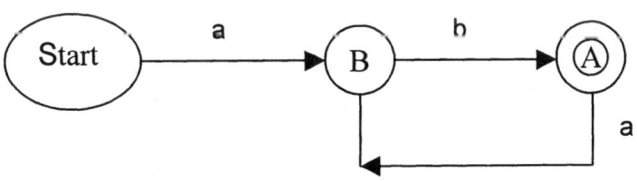

Figure 12.
The capitalized symbols in circles are state names, the lower case

41

symbols are from the machine's alphabet. These latter symbols label state transitions, and can be thought of as being either emitted or consumed, depending on whether the machine is being used for generation or recognition. The state A in the double circle is the *accepting* state of the machine, meaning that when in this state the machine has generated (or recognized) a valid string of L. Finite-state machines have no external storage, nor any memory save for their states, which by definition are finite in number. Hence it is clear that one cannot be used for recognizing palindromes, since the 'forward-sequence' part of the palindrome can be arbitrarily long before its inverse needs be considered.

It can be easily proved that for every regular grammar there is a corresponding FSM, and vice-versa.[10] Just as there are constraints on FSMs, so there are constraints on Type 3 grammars.[11] By successively relaxing these constraints, we get successively more powerful sets of grammars and machines. Type 0 grammars are called *unrestricted* since the productions can have any combination of terminal and non-terminal symbols on the left and right sides. The machines they correspond to are precisely the Turing machines!

Computer programming languages are almost exclusively Type 2 or context-free languages. The lexical and syntactical analysis components of compilers[12] are known as parsers, and have been studied for years. Their properties are well-liked and understood in the computer-science community, and it is tempting to use them to describe language. For example, the simple scheme of productions in Figure 13 might seem to be a good start at describing English:

> Sentence → NounPhrase VerbPhrase
> VerbPhrase → IntransVerb |[13] TransVerb NounPhrase
> NounPhrase → Determiner Adjective*[14] Noun
> Determiner → "a" | "the"
> Noun → "boy" | "girl" | "dog" | ...
> TransVerb → "likes" | ...
> ....

Figure 13.

However, nobody has thus far been able to come up with a complete grammar of English (or any other natural language), whether as Type 2, Type 1 (context-sensitive) or Type 0. This is partly due to the sheer complexity of a language with hundreds of thousands of terminal strings, and partly due to constraints imposed by semantics. In fact, it is not known what the Type of English is; it has not even been formally proved that English must be at least a Type 0, although it is suspected that it must be. Turing viewed the human brain as a machine, an enormously complicated one perhaps, but a machine with states, inputs, outputs and transition rules. Since, by definition, the human brain is capable of generating and recognizing English, and since any computable operation can be simulated by a Turing machine, then English must be at worst a Type 0 language.[15] We will return to the issue of language in a later chapter.

Endnotes

[1] Turing (1948) p. 13 mentions the learning of languages as one of a number of challenges (including games such as chess, tic-tac-toe, bridge and poker; language translation; cryptography and mathematics) which may be suitable for a machine to demonstrate intelligence, but dismisses it thus:

> Of the above possible fields the learning of languages would be the most impressive, since it is the most human of these activities. This field seems however to depend rather too much on sense organs and locomotion to be feasible.

[2] Hodges (1983), pp. 152-154.

[3] The ability of words to have multiple meanings even in normal circumstances – for example "lead", which means to go in front, and also is the name of a metallic element.

[4] It also makes for considerable difficulties in communication between humans!

[5] Turing (1953).

[6] Turing (1945).

[7] The bare word "computer" at that time referred to the human operator.

[8] And in a sense neither did general linguistics. It did not merit even an index entry in the 1944 Encyclopædia Britannica, because at the time the field was known as philology.

[9] There are many ways to set up the productions for a given language. The one given here is not the simplest, but corresponds directly to its equivalent finite-state machine given below.

---

[10] See Hopcroft and Ullman, Chapter 9.

[11] e.g. that there is always a single non-terminal on the left-hand side of a production, and the right-hand side has a single terminal symbol with a possible non-terminal on the left (or right) of it.

[12] Software programs which analyze and convert other programs written in a computer language into the base machine code of the computer on which the program is to run.

[13] The vertical bar, indicating "OR", is a syntactic shorthand. A production "A → B | C" could equally well be written as the two productions "A → B" and "A → C".

[14] This is the "Kleene Star", a syntactic shorthand to indicate 0, 1 or more repetitions of the starred quantity.

[15] This of course only follows if one thinks of the brain as a machine, which Turing did. Chomsky would strongly disagree – for him the brain is an organ with innate capabilities transcending the mechanical.

5

The Turing Test

What is intelligence? Can all humans think? Can animals think? If so, can all species think? Is language required for thinking, or is thinking required for language, or is there no connection? These and similar questions have been debated by philosophers for centuries. However, it is only in recent times that the question: can machines think? has been reasonable to pose. With the transformation of computers from enormous adding machines to general purpose devices – albeit a far cry from what we have today – in the middle of the 20th century, it became plausible to consider that computers could actually exhibit some of the mental behaviors of their human creators. While it might have been a question of idle intellectual curiosity to most, to those such as Turing in the forefront of the new subject of Computer Science and what was to become Artificial Intelligence it was a serious issue.

Turing avoided directly answering the question of intelligence by trying to define it explicitly. Instead he devised an *operational* definition by which the performance of a machine could be compared with that of a human at tasks presumed to require intelligence. This procedure was described in the article *Computing Machinery and Intelligence* Turing published in Mind in 1950. This test has since been known as the Turing Test, and has become established as the standard working criterion for intelligence in machines.

The test is in the form of a guessing game. The participant known as the interrogator must attempt to guess the sexes of two other players, hidden from the first participant, by means of a series of questions and answers transmitted through a teletype-like interface. The initial formulation of the problem is that of starting with a man and a woman, both trying to persuade the interrogator that each is the woman. Turing asks if the woman's place were taken by a computer, how would the interrogator fare? If the machine has achieved human-like intelligence, the interrogator should guess wrongly as often as before.[1] Turing doesn't say so explicitly, but some assume that he intended that when the machine takes the place of the man, the nature of the game changes to that of distinguishing between human and computer, and that the remaining human participant can be of either sex. Collins argues that societal changes over the years have made the change moot, but a machine would have a relatively easy time imitating a 1950's man imitating a woman, since men then did not share much in women's lives.[2] In any case, it is the modified interpretation of the game that has been adopted in the field as the canonical test for intelligence; there is presumably little difference in the degree or kind of intelligence required by a successful player in either formulation, and so we will adopt the second form too.

We reproduce here the first section of Turing's paper.

I propose to consider the question, 'Can machines think? ' This should begin with definitions of the meaning of the terms 'machine' and 'think'. The definitions might be framed so as to reflect so far as possible the normal use of the words, but this attitude is dangerous, If the meaning of the words 'machine' and "think" are to be found by examining how they are commonly used it is difficult to escape the conclusion that the meaning and the answer to the question, 'Can machines think? ' is to be sought in a statistical survey such as a Gallup poll. But this is absurd. Instead of attempting such a definition I shall replace the question by another, which is closely related to it and is expressed in relatively unambiguous words.

The new form of the problem can be described in terms of a game which we call the 'imitation game'. It is played with three people, a man (A), a woman (B), and an interrogator (C) who may be of either sex. The interrogator stays in a room apart front the other two. The object of the game for the interrogator is to determine which of the other two is the man and which is the woman. He knows them by labels X and Y, and at the end of the game he says either 'X is A and Y is B' or

'X is B and Y is A'. The interrogator is allowed to put questions to A and B thus:

C: Will X please tell me the length of his or her hair?

Now suppose X is actually A, then A must answer. It is A's object in the game to try and cause C to make the wrong identification. His answer might therefore be:

'My hair is shingled, and the longest strands are about nine inches long'.

In order that tones of voice may not help the interrogator the answers should be written, or better still, typewritten. The ideal arrangement is to have a teleprinter communicating between the two rooms. Alternatively the question and answers can be repeated by an intermediary. The object of the game for the third player (B) is to help the interrogator. The best strategy for her is probably to give truthful answers. She can add such things as 'I am the woman, don't listen to him! ' to her answers, but it will avail nothing as the man can make similar remarks.

We now ask the question, 'What will happen when a machine takes the part of A in this game? ' Will the interrogator decide wrongly as often when the game is played like this as he does when the game is played between a man and a woman? These questions replace our original, 'Can machines think? '

Hofstadter[3] points out that a success for the man in the original imitation game does not prove that the man was a woman, and so asks what exactly is the analogy to be made. This is not a problem. If the man prevails in the original game, he will have successfully shown that woman-like behavior (at least the verbal behavior that is the subject of the test) as performed by a man is indistinguishable as to sex from that performed by a woman. The analogy with the Turing test is direct: a success for the computer will mean that the "thinking" behavior as performed by the computer is indistinguishable from the thinking (no quotes) behavior performed by a human.

Turing does not explicitly state what he is claiming is the relationship between the ability of machines to think and the ability to pass the test. It is commonly taken that passing the test is a sufficient demonstration that thinking at the human level has been achieved. Technically this leaves open the possibility that human thinking is possible in a machine which can still not pass the test.

One might argue that on the spectrum of thinking, where one end is occupied by the brightest of humanity and the other by a rock, that the gap between the point representing minimum human intelligence and that representing the intelligence to pass the Turing test is small enough to be not worth considering. However, we run into some small difficulties when we consider the test – either form, in fact – taking place with someone from a very different culture – say a Xhosa tribesman who has been taught English but knows precious little of Western culture. To be even more dramatic, one might consider an interplanetary traveller, an alien with surely at least as much intelligence as human but no knowledge of Earthly ways, and an unknown complement of emotions. It becomes clear that passing the test cannot possibly be a necessary condition for intelligence, but must remain merely a sufficient one.

Playing Devil's Advocate

After presenting the imitation game, Turing immediately proceeds to present an opening critique of the set-up:

> As well as asking, 'What is the answer to this new form of the question, ' one may ask, "Is this new question a worthy one to investigate?" This latter question we investigate without further ado, thereby cutting short an infinite regress.

> The new problem has the advantage of drawing a fairly sharp line between the physical and the intellectual capacities of a man. No engineer or chemist claims to be able to produce a material which is indistinguishable from the human skin. It is possible that at some time this might be done, but even supposing this invention available we should feel there was little point in trying to make a 'thinking machine' more human by dressing it up in such artificial flesh. The form in which we have set the problem reflects this fact in the condition which prevents the interrogator from seeing or touching the other competitors, or hearing -their voices. Some other advantages of the proposed criterion may be shown up by specimen questions and answers. Thus:

> Q: Please write me a sonnet on the subject of the Forth Bridge.

> A : Count me out on this one. I never could write poetry.

Q: Add 34957 to 70764.

A: (Pause about 30 seconds and then give as answer) 105621.

Q: Do you play chess?

A: Yes.

Q: I have K at my K1, and no other pieces. You have only K at K6 and R at R1. It is your move. What do you play?

A: (After a pause of 15 seconds) R-R8 mate.

The question and answer method seems to be suitable for introducing almost any one of the fields of human endeavour that we wish to include. We do not wish to penalise the machine for its inability to shine in beauty competitions, nor to penalise a man for losing in a race against an aeroplane. The conditions of our game make these disabilities irrelevant. The 'witnesses' can brag, if they consider it advisable, as much as they please about their charms, strength or heroism, but the interrogator cannot demand practical demonstrations.

The game may perhaps be criticised on the ground that the odds are weighted too heavily against the machine. If the man were to try and pretend to be the machine he would clearly make a very poor showing. He would be given away at once by slowness and inaccuracy in arithmetic. May not machines carry out something which ought to be described as thinking but which is very different from what a man does? This objection is a very strong one, but at least we can say that if, nevertheless, a machine can be constructed to play the imitation game satisfactorily, we need not be troubled by this objection.

It might be urged that when playing the 'imitation game' the best strategy for the machine may possibly be something other than imitation of the behaviour of a man. This may be, but I think it is unlikely that there is any great effect of this kind. In any case there is no intention to investigate here the theory of the game, and it will be assumed that the best strategy is to try to provide answers that would naturally be given by a man.

While at Cambridge, Turing undoubtedly did his fair share of staying up till the small hours, sipping sherry or college port and

49

discussing with his fellow students all manner of matters of deep significance.[4] Despite the strong connection between mathematical logic and philosophy, he never wrote any papers from the standpoint of a philosopher: all his published writings were on mathematics, mathematical logic, computers, mechanical intelligence and, towards the end of his life, the morphogenesis of plants. However, he did understand the issues raised by his imitation game, and even anticipated some of the reactions it would receive. Being of a practical nature, he attempted a preemptive strike against his future detractors in the latter sections of *Computing Machinery and Intelligence*. His approach was to enumerate a series of objections, and to present his own counter-objections.

Objections

The first objection he notes is of a theological nature. Only beings with immortal souls could think, and since neither animals nor machines had souls, neither could think. He suggests that animals should be classified with men rather than machines, but the entire concern with animals is a red herring. The main fault he finds with this objection is that it would appear to limit God's power. He rejects this with the explanation that God would just be less likely to want to "confer a soul" on entities with insufficient brain power, but would not be absolutely constrained.

> In attempting to construct such machines we should not be irreverently usurping His power of creating souls, any more than we are in the procreation of children: rather we are, in either case, instruments of His will providing mansions for the souls that He creates.

Turing distances himself from too strong an identification with this view, but feels a need to provide a reaction to a theological argument in like terms. A related argument is what Turing calls the "Heads in the Sand" objection. People like, even need, to believe that mankind is superior to all other species. The mere possibility of this not being so is threatening to some; he suggests more to intellectuals than to others, since they value intellectual thought more. He concludes:

I do not think that this argument is sufficiently substantial to require refutation. Consolation would be more appropriate: perhaps this should be sought in the transmigration of souls.

Turing doesn't pursue this line of thought, making his exact intent open to conjecture. As a mathematical argument, though, Turing uses his own work as a straw man, namely that there are certain questions which cannot be answered mechanically:

> The questions that we know the machine must fail on are of this type, "Consider the machine specified as follows. . . . Will this machine ever answer 'Yes' to any question?" The dots are to be replaced by a description of some machine in standard form ...

The force of this argument is that machines have a certain disability to which humans are immune. Turing's counter-argument is that it has never been explicitly established that humans don't suffer from the same disability.

In an earlier paper,[5] he approaches the mathematical objection rather differently, addressing the making of mistakes:

> The argument from Gödel's and other theorems ... rests essentially on the condition that the machine must not make mistakes. But this is not a requirement for intelligence. It is related that the infant Gauss was asked at school to do the addition $15 + 18 + 21 + ... + 54$ (or something of the kind) and that he immediately wrote down 483, presumably having calculated it as $(15 + 54)(54 - 12)/2.3$. One can imagine circumstances where a foolish master told the child that he ought instead to have added 18 to 15 obtaining 33, then added 21, etc. From some points of view this would be a 'mistake', in spite of the obvious intelligence involved. One can also imagine a situation where the children were given a number of additions to do, of which the first 5 were all arithmetic progressions, but the 6th was say $23 + 34 + 45 + ... + 100 + 112 + 122 + ... + 199$. Gauss might have given the answer to this as if it were an arithmetic progression, not having noticed that the 9th term was 112 instead of 111. This would be a definite mistake, which the less intelligent children would not

51

have been likely to make.

What Turing calls an "argument from consciousness" would perhaps better be called an argument from emotion: no machine can exhibit in a believable manner all (or even any) of the gamut of emotions humans are capable of. He does not directly argue this point either way, but points out that we cannot tell *for sure* that another human being actually has emotions or is capable of thought, except by being that person. Since people adopt the "polite convention that everyone thinks," they should likewise give him the benefit of the doubt.

He combines a number of objections under the heading of "arguments from various disabilities", being various attributes and characteristics that are assumed to be uniquely human (or at least of a biological being). Perhaps the most intriguing of these is the objection that a machine could never be the subject of its own thought. This is the closest Turing comes to analyzing in this paper what for some is a definition of consciousness. Hofstadter, for example, argues[6] that having a symbol for one's self in one's mental repertoire is required for consciousness.[7] Turing argues that the objection can be nullified merely by showing that the machine has some thought with some subject matter. He argues that if the machine is solving a quadratic equation, for example, then that equation would be part of the machine's subject matter. Granted, but this argument avoids whether the machine is actually thinking. Turing recovers immediately with some predictions that get to the core of the advances in programming and thinking about programming that are introduced with the new field of artificial intelligence.

> It may be used to help in making up its own programmes, or to predict the effect of alterations in its own structure. By observing the results of its own behaviour it can modify its own programmes so as to achieve some purpose more effectively. These are possibilities of the near future, rather than Utopian dreams.

What is Surprise?

We will consider further Turing's contributions to AI in a later section. What Turing terms "Lady Lovelace's objection" comes from Ada, Countess Lovelace, colleague of Charles Babbage and probably the world's first software engineer. She said of the Analytical Engine that it could never originate anything, that it "could do whatever we know how to order it to perform." Turing had previously[8] written:

> The view ... that intelligence in machinery is merely a reflection of that of its creator is rather similar to the view that the credit for the discoveries of a pupil should be given to his teacher. In such a case the teacher would be pleased with the success of his methods of education, but would not claim the results themselves unless he had actually communicated them to his pupil. He would certainly have envisaged in very broad outline the sort of thing his pupil might be expected to do, but would not expect to foresee any sort of detail. It is already possible to produce machines where this sort of situation arises in a small degree. One can produce 'paper machines' for playing chess. Playing against such a machine gives a definite feeling that one is pitting one's wits against something alive.

Note in the quote above from Lady Lovelace the absence of the word "only". Turing picked up on that and suggested the variant objection that computers could do nothing new, and that they cannot take humans by surprise. This he counters with his own experience with computers (which is more than that of 99.99...% of the world at that time), that they take him by surprise all the time. A detractor might assert that surprise is due to a creative mental act by the observer, but according to Turing that mental act is no greater when it is a machine that elicits the surprise than when anything or anyone else does. That is, just because it requires cognitive ability to be surprised should not in itself diminish the act that caused the surprise in the first place.

If one allows that one form of surprise is to enjoy a joke, then it can be demonstrated easily that machines can surprise humans by providing an algorithmic procedure for generating jokes. Children's jokes are particularly amenable to this approach, because of their inherently formulaic character. This does not lessen their relevance to this problem, since *any* ability to evoke a smile or even a groan in an adult will suffice to demolish the objection. Consider the following joke:

Q. Why do hummingbirds hum?

A. Because they don't know the words.

This can be analysed into the following outline program.

Enumerate all animals.[9]
For each animal A, enumerate its significant behavioral
   actions.[10]
Choose an action B_A that is something also associated with
   humans.
Establish a reason $R_{B,A}$ why humans might not want or be
   able to perform action B_A.
Construct a joke in the form:
   Q. Why do As B_A?
   A. Because they $R_{B,A}$.

For example:
Q. Why do birds fly?
A. Because they get motion sickness on the train.

The procedure given above is an example of the *effective procedure* described in chapter 3, subject to the considerations mentioned in the Endnotes. The interested reader is encouraged to try to follow the procedure with his/her own values, and judge how surprising the results may be.

In the early days of artificial intelligence research, in fact in the early days of computer science, there was much interest in the topic of automatic theorem proving, in particular proving theorems from geometry. The field was attractive to investigators because it lent itself well to formalization: the geometrical figures concerned could be represented by a collection of logical axioms regarding lengths of line segments, angles and connectedness, and the geometrical axioms and theorems could be represented as rules of inference. More importantly, the field seemed to embody the requirements of logical thought, and the steps of an automatic proof procedure would correspond directly to the steps a human might make in solving the same problem (as distinct from the inherent inscrutability of the neural networks that were to follow). In other words, these are the kinds of problems that humans solve at the cognitive level.

It was never expected that machines could derive proofs that were particularly original. The methodology employed was essentially and entirely one of search. The machine would start with a set of assertions or axioms, and each application of an inference rule would generate a conclusion which was added to the set of assertions. The challenge was to get the right rules applied in the right sequence; it would by no means necessarily be fatal if an undesired rule were attempted: maybe it would fail to conclude anything, or maybe it would generate a conclusion that was true but irrelevant to the task in hand. If the correct and sufficient axioms were supplied initially, and the appropriate inference rules were available, then the only issue was whether the machine would be able to finish the proof in a reasonable time. The two possible reasons for failure would be (1) following some lengthy correct but irrelevant path which kept branching so that the proof never got back to an earlier alternative, or (2) got into a loop. It was one of the difficulties that developers of these programs faced to build in "meta-logic" to their proof mechanisms to detect and avoid such situations.

The programs of the late 50's and sixties were certainly able to achieve the competence of a high-school geometer or better. Indeed, a group led by H. Gelernter claimed of their program:

> If the interrogator were to restrict his probing to the area of theorem-proving in elementary Euclidean plane geometry, our machine could be expected to give an excellent account of itself in competition with a human in Turing's well-known "imitation game".[11]

Their program[12] was able to produce proofs that were not expected by the designers, but this fact alone was not surprising, given that many if not all geometric problems can be tackled from several different directions. However, a program by Marvin Minsky, not described as fully in the literature but believed to employ the same principles as Gelernter's program, did produce a proof that surprised many observers.

As well as standard theorems that we all learn explicitly when learning geometry in school, Gelernter's program was given a set of rules to exploit symmetry and overcome arbitrary naming conventions. These correspond to the "common sense" rules that humans bring to bear upon such problems. For example, there may be a rule that if angle ABC is 90° then ABC is a right triangle – but what if angle BCA is 90°? In order to avoid making duplicates of all of the rules to cover all possible permutations of the arguments, these extra rules of symmetry were used to advantage.

Gelernter's program was able to make constructions (i.e. line-segments added to the original geometric diagram to aid in the proof), but despite being necessary in some cases, these constructions made the general problem more difficult since at each step of operation there were that many more possibilities to try, and the overall search space became significantly larger.

Now, the standard proof that an isosceles triangle ABC (that is, one with two equal sides AB and AC) has two equal angles ABC and ACB, involves a construction, namely dropping a perpendicular from the vertex A to the base at D. The simple proof then uses the facts that AB = AC, angles ADB and ADC are equal and AD is common to prove that triangles ABD and ACD are congruent, so angle ABC must equal ACB (see Figure 14a).

Minsky's program, was able to construct a novel proof that didn't involve a construction; this proof had apparently not been known in modern times. According to Donald Michie, one of the pioneers of artificial intelligence and a former colleague of Alan Turing's at Bletchley Park, "It is also shorter and simpler than Euclid's, and has an additional quality which the impartial geometer might well describe as 'brilliance'."[13]

The proof was as follows. Side AB = AC. Side AC = AB. Angle BAC = angle CAB. Therefore triangles ABC and ACB are congruent, so angle ABC = ACB (see Figure 14b).

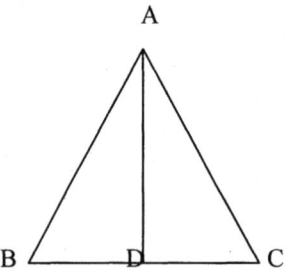

Figure 14.a

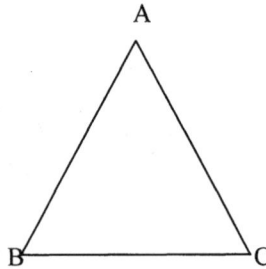

Figure 14b

What the program did that was so unexpected was to treat triangle ABC and its reflection ACB as different entities! While the final result was unexpected, every single step of operation of the machine, i.e. every step in the proof, was one that was taken from the repertoire programmed into it. In particular, the symmetry rules allowed the particular proof to be found. It is not that humans are unaware of properties of reflection – indeed such devices are commonly used in geometry – it is just that no-one had happened to use that technique at that point in the proof of that particular problem before. The proof, once seen, seems so obvious, and its simplicity makes it particularly elegant. All the program did was to apply its rules to the initial conditions, and some combination of chance and design in the ordering of the rules to be attempted caused the new proof to be found before the traditional one. The performance of these programs, which were operating just a few years after Turing's death, would have given Turing much satisfaction.

Further Objections

Another objection that Turing considers is what he calls the "argument from continuity in the nervous system", namely that one cannot simulate the behavior of a continuous system with a discrete-state machine. While that may be true in principle, Turing argues that the computer can still behave in a way that the interrogator would never be able to tell. He suggests that a digital device can mimic an analog one by responding to questions requiring a certain numerical value, not with that value but with one chosen from a range around the correct value, according to a probability distribution akin to the normal distribution. In doing so he anticipates future inventions such as probabilistic finite state automata and pattern recognition by hidden Markov models.

The "argument from informality of behaviour" addresses the issue of whether it is possible to enshrine in a collection of rules enough guidance to enable humans to function in all possible likely and unlikely circumstances of life. Turing states:

> It is not possible to produce a set of rules purporting to describe what a man should do in every conceivable set of circumstances. One might for instance have a rule that one is to stop when one sees a red traffic light, and to go if one sees a green one, but what if by some fault both appear together? One may perhaps decide that it is safest to stop. But some further difficulty may well arise from this decision later. To attempt to provide rules of conduct to cover every eventuality, even those arising from traffic lights, appears to be impossible. With all this I agree.

> From this it is argued that we cannot be machines. I shall try to reproduce the argument, but I fear I shall hardly do it justice. It seems to run something like this. 'If each man had a definite set of rules of conduct by which he regulated his life

> he would be no better than a machine. But there are no such
> rules, so men cannot be machines.' The undistributed middle
> is glaring. I do not think the argument is ever put quite like
> this, but I believe this is the argument used nevertheless.
> There may however be a certain confusion between 'rules of
> conduct' and 'laws of behaviour' to cloud the issue. By 'rules
> of conduct' I mean precepts such as 'Stop if you see red
> lights', on which one can act, and of which one can be
> conscious. By 'laws of behaviour' I mean laws of nature as
> applied to a man's body such as 'if you pinch him he will
> squeak'. If we substitute 'laws of behaviour which regulate
> his life' for 'laws of conduct by which he regulates his life' in
> the argument quoted the undistributed middle is no longer
> insuperable. For we believe that it is not only true that being
> regulated by laws of behaviour implies being some sort of
> machine (though not necessarily a discrete-state machine), but
> that conversely being such a machine implies being regulated
> by such laws. However, we cannot so easily convince
> ourselves of the absence of complete laws of behaviour as of
> complete rules of conduct. The only way we know of for
> finding such laws is scientific observation, and we certainly
> know of no circumstances under which we could say, 'We
> have searched enough. There are no such laws.'

Turing's "rules of conduct" would seem to correspond with cognitive behaviour, whereas his "laws of behaviour" would correspond with subcognitive behaviour. He argues here that the latter are suitable for "regulation by", i.e. implementation on a machine, but that the former aren't. He does not say that the rules of conduct are not *in principle* unimplementable on a machine, or even that implementing some would not be straightforward, but rather that the scale of the enterprise makes achieving complete coverage in practice unlikely.

Turing's final argument is that from Extra-Sensory Perception (ESP). Turing believes, albeit reluctantly, that there is sufficient evidence to take claims of ESP seriously. However, the specifics of the objection, namely that some humans are telepathic, and so will be able to outperform computers at the standard ESP card-guessing games. This argument is dispatched quickly with the observation that "With ESP anything may happen,"[14] i.e. that maybe parts of computers could be sensitive to telepathy too.

The number and breadth of the objections Turing lists suggests that he has encountered at least some of them in discussions with his colleagues. There is a slight undertone of impatience, suggesting he does not suffer fools gladly (although he concedes that some of the enumerated objections are more worthy than others); this may be related to his difficulties, mentioned earlier, with getting along at NPL.

Endnotes

---

[1] Turing quantifies the performance thus: "I believe that in about fifty years' time it will be possible to programme computers, with a storage capacity of 10^9, to make them play the imitation game so well that an average interrogator will not have more than 70 per cent. chance of making the correct identification after five minutes of questioning." His measure of 10^9 digits corresponds to about 400 megabytes.

[2] Collins (1990) p. 182. His entire chapter 13 is devoted to discussing sociological problems with the test, and ways in which the protocol can be modified to make the test more rigorous.

[3] "The Turing Test: A Coffeehouse Conversation" published as chapter 5 of Hofstadter & Dennett (1981)

[4] The reader who is curious about Cambridge lifestyles might enjoy Tom Sharpe's hilariously funny novel *Porterhouse Blue* (Prentice Hall, 1974), about a fictional (but highly believable) Cambridge college.

[5] Turing (1948).

[6] Hofstadter (1979).

[7] Although the reverse is not true. Some of the earliest AI programs, such as that which controlled the SRI International robot Shakey had representations of themselves, but could hardly be called conscious.

[8] Turing (1948).

[9] Actually, it's not necessary to be so complete. Simply to list all, or even a number of, the animals in a children's animal book will be sufficient.

[10] It might at first sight look as if deep understanding of human and animal behavior is required to fulfill these steps. However, a simple listing of these characteristics is all that is required. There are currently many on-line dictionaries, thesauri and ontologies that information of a kind similar what would be required by a computer executing this program.

[11] Gelernter et al. (1960).

[12] Gelernter (1959).

---

[13] Michie (1974), p. 5.

[14] Not unlike the fact that in mathematical logic, anything can be proven from a single contradiction.

6

The Turing Test Tested

There are other objections to the Turing test beyond the ones Turing himself enumerates. One of the problems that has plagued artificial intelligence is that of the need for general or common knowledge. The major fields in AI, such as natural language understanding, vision, planning and so on, continually run into trouble when explored through the medium of *toy worlds* because the programs developed to exhibit some new approach to the subject lack any background knowledge, any "common sense".

Now, one of the most successful areas of artificial intelligence, indeed the only one that has met with any appreciable commercial success to date, is that of *expert systems*. Expert systems basically consist of one of a variety of types of inference engine, plus a collection of rules. The basic operation of the expert system is as follows. A problem is posed to it in a suitable formalism, certain rules will match and hence 'fire', which through the inference engine will cause other rules to fire, and so on until a conclusion is reached.[1] A typical domain suitable for expert systems would be that of medical diagnosis, say of tropical diseases or forms of cancer. The program will be given the relevant symptoms and other medical observations and measurements, and will proceed through what is essentially a decision-tree traversal, although it might involve maximizing probabilities (confidences) of each traversal. Each inferencing step in the program's operation can be thought of corresponding to a step in the physician's own thought processes ("if the patient's blood count for a substance is so-and-so, then it is likely he is unable to metabolize such-and-such..."). Indeed, a major component in the production of the expert system is the involvement of the knowledge engineer, typically a computer scientist conversant in the field who interviews one or more experts in an attempt to capture their decision processes. Two things should be noted: (1) it is only the thinking processes which the expert is able to introspect on and articulate that can get captured by this method, and (2) for these programs to work, no deep understanding of the domain nor any general knowledge of the world is required. A medical diagnosis program does not know what a disease actually is, and would totally fail any Turing test that veered from a precisely controlled dialogue concerning the domain in question.

Strong AI

There are differences in opinion amongst AI researchers and interested observers of the field as to the extent to which AI, as implemented today through computer programs, does or can approach the "minimum requirements" for a working brain. It is clear to all that the brain is sufficient for intelligence, thinking, understanding – all of the cognitive abilities that AI attempts to reproduce in a machine – but there is no consensus whether it is necessary. Broadly speaking, there are two schools of thought on this matter. Proponents of "Weak AI" would argue that the computer is an invaluable tool for the simulation of models of cognitive processing, but do not go all the way to say that a machine in turn can go all the way to simulate a human brain. Proponents of "Strong AI", on the other hand, would say that there is nothing essential about the brain for the effecting of cognitive processes. They would say that any operation that is implemented in hardware can be simulated in software, and hence that a computer could, suitably programmed, perform any cognitive activity. In other words, a computer could have mental states, and there would be no intrinsic difference between these states and those of a real brain, save the physical substrate.

If a computer could pass the Turing test, there would be no operational way to distinguish it from a human. It would have to have instantaneous internal configurations that could not be told apart functionally from human mental states. Thus a proponent of Strong AI would readily believe it to be possible to have a computer pass the Turing test. As Penrose says,[2] it would depend on the equivalence of universal Turing machines and the fact that any algorithm can be effected by such a machine (c.f. the Church-Turing thesis) and the presumption that the brain acts according to some kind of algorithmic action. This latter point is clearly true as far as the cognitive steps of which we are consciously aware are concerned, but must be taken on faith for subcognitive processing.[3]

There are proponents and detractors of the Strong AI view from many different academic fields. In order to explore the validity of the Turing test as any kind of measure of intelligence, we single out the philosopher John Searle as principal detractor, and examine his views and those of his own rebutters in some detail. Searle, as well as others such as Hubert Dreyfus,[4] argue philosophically that symbol manipulation cannot be the basis of human intelligence. This is not to pretend there are no other approaches to the problem; for example, the Nobel Prize-winning neuroscientist Gerald Edelman has written compellingly that the mental activity we know as the mind is the consequence of physics, biology, morphological evolution and selection and could not possibly be embodied in computer programs.[5] The problem with introducing such arguments here are twofold: first, being from a basis in neuroscience, they do not deal with Turing's proposal on its own terms, and second, they ultimately cannot disprove that mechanical intelligence is possible, but rather only explain why neural intelligence can exist. Hence we turn to Searle.

Searle's Chinese Room

One of the major critics of the Turing test as means of determining whether thinking or understanding has taken place is John Searle. In 1980 he published a paper[6] which caused a firestorm of activity in the largely academic on-line AI mailing lists and discussion groups, with heated arguments on both sides (but predominantly anti-Searle). We will examine Searle's argument in some detail because it considers precisely the kind of dialogue that Turing supposes a machine capable of passing his test could undergo.

Searle chose to use as his central discussion point the work of Roger Schank,[7] a computer scientist then at Yale. Schank had developed the notion of a *script* as an AI knowledge representation format suitable for the understanding of simple stories.[8] Quoting from Searle,

> Very briefly, and leaving out the various details, one can describe Schank's program as follows: The aim of the program is to simulate the human ability to understand stories.

63

It is characteristic of human beings' story-understanding capacity that they can answer questions about the story even though the information that they give was never explicitly stated in the story. Thus, for example, suppose you are given the following story: "A man went into a restaurant and ordered a hamburger. When the hamburger arrived it was burned to a crisp, and the man stormed out of the restaurant angrily, without paying for the hamburger or leaving a tip." Now, if you are asked "Did the man eat the hamburger?" you will presumably answer, "No, he did not." Similarly, if you are given the following story: "A man went into a restaurant and ordered a hamburger; when the hamburger came he was very pleased with it; and as he left the restaurant he gave the waitress a large tip before paying his bill," and you are asked the question, "Did the man eat the hamburger?" you will presumably answer, "Yes, he ate the hamburger." Now Schank's machines can similarly answer questions about restaurants in this fashion. To do this, they have a "representation" of the sort of information that human beings have about restaurants, which enables them to answer such questions as those above, given these sorts of stories. When the machine is given the story and then asked the question, the machine will print out answers of the sort that we would expect human beings to give if told similar stories. Partisans of strong AI claim that in this question and answer sequence the machine is not only simulating a human ability but also (1) that the machine can literally be said to understand the story and provide the answers to questions, and (2) that what the machine and its program do explains the human ability to understand the story and answer questions about it.

To discredit the beliefs of Strong AI proponents, Searle introduces what has come to be called his Chinese Room. He supposes that he, a native English speaker who knows no Chinese at all, is locked in a room. He is provided with sets of instructions which tell him how to manipulate Chinese characters (which to him are just squiggles, devoid of meaning). He is provided with some text in Chinese (namely questions about a story) and through manipulations according to the instructions he is to generate a set of symbols (the answers to said questions). He argues that given sufficiently accurate and plentiful instructions, he can achieve a level of performance at answering questions about the story that are indistinguishable from that of a native

Chinese speaker's, yet he remains totally ignorant of the story in particular and Chinese in general – indeed he is even unaware that the input is a set of questions and the output contains answers.

He concludes from this thought experiment that since he, in his Chinese room, understands nothing of Chinese or the story, that a computer such as Schank's would understand nothing too. In other words, he maintains that operational performance of putative cognitive tasks is not a determiner of understanding. In fact, he goes further. He maintains that no machine that operates entirely by the formal manipulation of symbols – which includes all man-made digital computers, whether electronic or not – can be said to understand anything.

Like Turing in *Computing Machinery and Intelligence*, Searle includes in his paper several anticipated counter-arguments to his proposals, along with his own rebuttals to them. The only one that we will examine here is the argument that Searle considers first, namely the "systems argument". In summary, the argument goes that it doesn't matter if the man in the Chinese room understands Chinese at all, it is the totality of the symbol processing system – the man, the symbols and the instructions – that achieves the understanding. Searle rejects this argument by supposing that the man memorizes all of the symbols and instructions so that the entirety of the question-and-answer task takes place within his head, yet he still understands no Chinese. This position can be attacked on several fronts; we will first ask exactly what "understanding" is.

According to Daniel Dennett,[9] the definitive rebuttal of Searle's argument is by Douglas Hofstadter.[10] Here Hofstadter argues strongly for the very "systems argument" that Searle attempts to dispose of, but in a way that makes a very strong case. Indeed, he asserts that Searle has been unable (or unwilling) to make a substantial answer to his (Hofstadter's) case. Hofstadter's argument runs roughly as follows.

Hofstadter's primary point is that Searle totally overlooks the magnitude of the task of having the human in the room   what Hofstadter calls *Searle's demon* – internalize the entire Chinese story understanding program. Hofstadter asserts that the entire set of *a priori* instructions for manipulating any (unseen) set of input Chinese symbols representing a question in order to give a response ascribable to a native Chinese speaker would likely occupy millions of pages and take a century to execute. This is probably a conservative estimate.

Hofstadter could have made some additional points. The enormous magnitude of the task of interpreting the story understanding program indicates that it was naïve to believe that Schank's program, or any reasonable improvement of it, could have come close to passing the Turing test. Sure, the story understanding that the program appeared to simulate would be necessary for passing the test, but it is far from sufficient. In other words, this does not negate the claims of Strong AI, but rather tells us that Strong AI proponents backed a weak and premature horse in Schank.

Another point that has been generally glossed over is that "understanding" in the abstract is not necessarily the same as "human understanding". After all, we take it for granted that while animals have some understanding of their environment, this understanding is not comparable to that of humans. The understanding of a child is not equivalent to that of an adult. Therefore it is conceivable that there are other kinds of understanding, maybe "superior" or maybe just different from adult understanding. The understanding that is central to the problem of the Chinese room is by definition human understanding, so is subject to the constraints that come with the human package. Although we are not necessarily able to quantify them, we know that there are limits to human memory – at least to the ability to memorize within a certain time – and to perform steps of reasoning. The interpretation task that Searle asks his demon to internalize is beyond human capability without the compilation process (learning) that accompanies understanding. Thus the scenario that is central to Searle's rebuttal of the systems argument is impossible, unless the demon has understood the problem.

Hofstadter points out that Searle has come down on the side of the "systems argument" in his response to his own detractors. In another thought experiment wherein there is a microscopic demon operating in a defective female brain, rushing around in picoseconds from synapse to synapse causing the required neural excitation for correct brain behaviour, Searle alleges it is the brain, not the demon, that possesses the human intelligence. By a clever mapping, Hofstadter sets up a correspondence between this case and the Chinese room, trapping Searle into being in favour of the systems argument for the latter situation too.

Despite the forcefulness and likely correctness of these lines of reasoning, a case can be made that they go overboard. Consider the basic objection, that the room does not "understand" Chinese. One need simply ask, for what end? There is no other activity in the universe of the room save for interpreting Chinese characters according to the scenario specified. There is no other situation contemplated, so there is no way to say that the room does not understand. The room performs exactly the same as a Chinese speaker would, so according to

Turing's operational definition, understanding has been achieved.

Intentionality

The essence of Searle's position is that there is no *intentionality* in the Chinese room, or any computer program that behaves by formal symbol manipulation; it cannot have intentional states if it lacks subjective experience The room (or program) does not *understand* anything; not the story, not what a hamburger is, not what any of the symbols mean, not what it is doing. The difficulty here, and this is not just an issue with Searle, is that it is not easy to define what understanding, even of a simple concept, consists of.

What is necessary for understanding of "hamburger" to be said to have taken place? A mental image? A set of descriptions of physical characteristics? A recipe? A set of descriptions of uses and circumstances in which one is to be found?

There are those who will argue that a machine can never understand physical objects of which it can have no direct experience. Indeed, Turing himself suggests this:[11]

> One way of setting about our task of building a 'thinking machine' would be to take a man as a whole and to try to replace all the parts of him by machinery. He would include television cameras, microphones, loudspeakers, wheels and 'handling servo-mechanisms' as well as some sort of 'electronic brain'. This would be a tremendous undertaking of course. The object, if produced by present techniques, would be of immense size, even if the 'brain' part were stationary and controlled the body from a distance. In order that the machine should have a chance of finding things out for itself it should be allowed to roam the countryside, and the danger to the ordinary citizen would be serious. Moreover even when the facilities mentioned above were provided, the creature would still have no contact with food, sex, sport and many other things of interest to the human being. Thus although this method is probably the 'sure' way of producing a thinking machine it seems to be altogether too slow and impracticable.

But then what about a simple arithmetic fact, such as 6*5=30? What does it mean to understand this? Is simply knowing it sufficient? To use a trick more normally reserved for more complicated products, you could say that if you moved the factor of two from the 6 to the 5, you get 3*10, which is easily calculated by adding a zero to the 3. Is this understanding? How about arranging 6 rows of 5 objects, and counting the collection?

We can address the quandary we are seemingly put in by Searle's construction by examining three other cognitive problems, which serve to highlight the inherent difficulty in making non-operational claims about understanding. These problems are from the fields of physics, recreational mathematics and linguistics. The ubiquity of this issue will serve to illustrate the inescapability of the notion that you cannot define understanding apart from its use.

A problem from Physics

In *Computing Machinery and Intelligence* Turing uses an interrogative dialog called *viva voce* to illustrate an interrogator questioning the other party's knowledge or understanding of a subject.

> Interrogator: In the first line of your sonnet which reads "Shall I compare thee to a summer's day," would not "a spring day" do as well or better?
>
> Witness: It wouldn't scan.
>
> Interrogator: How about "a winter's day," That would scan all right.
>
> Witness: Yes, but nobody wants to be compared to a winter's day.
>
> Interrogator: Would you say Mr. Pickwick reminded you of Christmas?
>
> Witness: In a way.
>
> Interrogator: Yet Christmas is a winter's day, and I do not think Mr. Pickwick would mind the comparison.
>
> Witness: I don't think you're serious. By a winter's day one means a typical winter's day, rather than a special one like Christmas.

This kind of questioning undoubtedly can separate full from rote learning, but a more depth-first approach may be more illustrative of when enough understanding is enough. Consider the following dialog, where the questioner can be anything from an inquisitive child to a probative professor.

Q: "Why is the sky blue?"
A: "Because of the Rayleigh effect"
Q: "What is that?"
A: "It concerns the scattering of light"
Q: "How?"
A: "Light rays of different frequencies are scattered to different degrees"
Q: "Why is that?"

And so on. It is clear that the questioning could proceed to the quantum level and eventually run up against the frontiers of current understanding. This does not mean that it is impossible for anyone to understand the answer to the original question, but rather that understanding has to be relative to some (actual or potential) use of the knowledge.

A Problem from Recreational Mathematics

The problem to be considered here in some detail is the well-known Tower of Hanoi.[12] In this problem, there are three vertical posts, and a collection of N circular discs of different diameters (no two being identical), and with holes bored in the centers to allow placement over the posts. (see Figure 15. This shows the problem with N=5 discs, but it can be set up with any number.) The discs are initially all on post A with the smallest on top, arranged in order of increasing size. The problem is to recreate the same arrangement on post B by moving the discs one at a time in the smallest number of moves, with the restriction that a disc may at no time rest on a smaller disc. This problem appears in puzzle books, is set as a programming exercise in introductory computer science classes, and even appears in somewhat disguised form as a task for the user in an interactive computer-based adventure game.[13]

Turing never mentioned the Tower of Hanoi problem in his writings, although he did think that analysis of games was a serious pursuit. He wrote a paper on the subject *Digital Computers Applied to Games*,[14] in which he focussed on chess (of which he was a keen but amateur-level player[15]), checkers[16] and nim.[17] This paper introduced many concepts and directions that researchers in AI were to seize upon and develop further. Indeed one of the first successful AI programs was Samuel's checkers program,[18] which owed much to Turing.

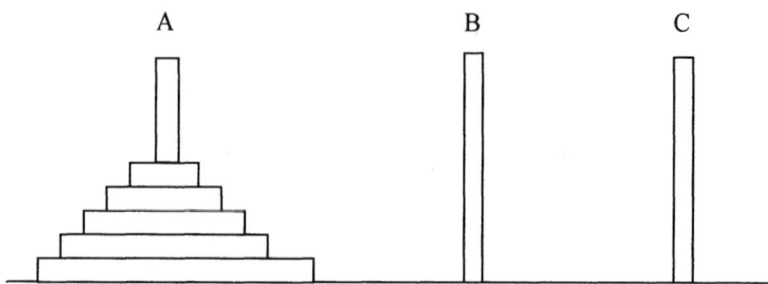

Figure 15.

If there are only two disks in our problem, the solution is trivial. The small disk is moved to post C, the large disk to post B, and the small disk back on top of the large disk. After a moment or two's reflection, the solution with N=3 is also discovered to be straightforward: the small disk moves to post B, the medium one to post C and then the small one onto the medium one. The large disk may now move to post B. Finally, the small disk is moved to post A, the medium disk to the large disk on post B, and then the small one back on top of the medium one. A moment or two's further reflection reveals what is going on.

There is a single process that is being repeated with different numbers of discs and different posts: to take a sub-pile of M discs from post X and move it to post Y using post Z as a temporary resting–place. (Here, X, Y and Z are used as *variables* and can stand for any of the posts A, B or C as appropriate.) The top-level problem of moving M disks from A to B is identical to the problem of moving the upper M of N (where M<N) disks from A to B (this is a sub-problem of the top-level problem of moving N disks from A to B), since the highest disk remaining on A is larger than any being moved, so may be treated as if it were the ground.

We may assert with some confidence that the explanation given above represents an understanding of the problem, although we will question this assertion shortly. So we now ask, What does it take to get a machine to understand the problem? Consider now the problem with 4 disks. We can break the problem into three sub-tasks.

Move the top 3 disks from A to C (we know how to do that).
Move the remaining disk from A to B.
Move the 3 disks on C over to B (we know how to do that).

It should be clear that the solution to the problem for any value of N can be given in terms of the solution for N-1. This allows mathematical proofs by induction to be generated, and also the creation of a *recursive* computer program – namely one that refers to itself. If we wish to write a program HANOI which takes 4 arguments – the number of disks to be moved, the name of the starting post, the name of the target post and the name of the third post which is used as an intermediate resting spot – and which prints out instructions to solve the problem, it might look like this:[19]

```
Program HANOI (integer N, string X, string Y, string Z) {
    HANOI (N-1, X, Z, Y);
    Print "Move disk from" X "to" Y;
    HANOI (N-1, Z, Y, X);
}
```

This is all it takes. Our program will be run for the initial configuration in Figure 15 by the invocation:

```
HANOI (5, "A", "B", "C")
```

A computer with the appropriate language compiler will be able to execute HANOI and produce the right results. But has the computer understood the problem? Yes and no. The computer clearly has a degree of competency in the problem, but has it understood it as well as the human? No, but then the tasks required were different. The computer was not required to take a description of the problem and generate a program that solved it, and solely with the program above it couldn't do that, so its understanding was clearly not at the same level as the human's.[20]

If we had a computer which could solve the problem from a statement of it in English, then we might test it in the following way. We might present it with a configuration that was an intermediate state in the solution of a problem and ask it to complete the task. Or we might present it with a legal configuration of disks, and ask it if the configuration is an intermediate state of the minimum-move solution to a problem. The computer might well fail in these tasks.[21] However, there is a good chance that a human, even one who has understood the recursive solution given above, would also fail. This should in no way invalidate the assumption of understanding of the simpler problem. Instead, it merely validates Turing's operational approach to understanding.

A Problem from Linguistics

The third illustration we will use is in the form of a couple of examples from linguistics. Recall the beginning of Lewis Carroll's Jabberwocky: "Twas brillig, and the slithy toves did gyre and gimble in the wabe". The poem is clearly gibberish, but from Carroll's clever use of portmanteau constructions for the *open-class* or *content words* of the language (the concrete nouns, verbs, adjectives and some adverbs) and by leaving the *closed-class* or *function words* (such as articles, conjunctions, prepositions) untouched, we get a feeling that we almost understand it. We can even confidently answer questions:

Q: "What were the weather conditions?"
A: "Brillig"
Q: "How would you describe the toves?"
A: "Slithy"

and so on. Of course, we have no certain knowledge what these words *mean*, but we know the roles they play in the poem.[22] We can imagine that at the very least, the Chinese Room could have the kind of understanding of Schank's scripts as we do of the Jabberwocky.

Now, understanding of language is something we all do, but it is frustratingly difficult to introspect how this understanding is achieved. For the content words, one can imagine that learning takes place at an early age by associating hearing the word in the context of its demonstration. ("Look at the doggie. Nice doggie.") The function words are more problematic, as are grammatical constructions and idioms.

A simple example from the world of idioms will further illustrate the difference between Turing's and Searle's concepts of understanding as applied to language. We will choose an example that is intermediate on a scale from commonplace to abstruse. Consider the phrase "jumping on the bandwagon".[23] It is not one of the first phrases we learn as children, and probably in many cases it is not taught or defined in school. People encounter it in written or spoken language and after a small number of instances have figured out its meaning from context, and are comfortable enough to use it, although almost certainly without any explicit Aha! experience. Very few people are probably aware of what the phrase means in the sense of how it is derived from its constituent words. They just know how to use it. By all reasonable, every-day interpretations of the word, these users would be asserted to *understand* the phrase. By Searle's argument, on the other hand, such people would not understand it at all (or most or all of the rest of language, by extension); Turing, of course, would have no problem.

All these examples serve to stress the point that Turing's operational definition of understanding stands up much better than the arguments of his principle detractor. John McCarthy has made use of the definition:

> Subject S understands knowledge K if S uses K when appropriate.

in his talks on AI. This very neatly captures the operational definition of understanding and summarizes in one sentence Turing's views.

Understanding via Learning

Finally, we can look at another aspect of Searle's argument that seems suspicious. He claims that while manipulating the Chinese symbols, he has no understanding of what he is doing. Well, it is a little hard to imagine this situation, since it is hard to imagine what these instructions would look like (i.e. the program to do story understanding to the degree that it would pass the Turing test). Let us suppose that the only task the room had to perform was to play tic-tac-toe.

The rules to win (or at least to guarantee a draw) at this game are few and easy to understand, and can be summarized thus:

> If it is your go, test for the following conditions in turn.
> If you can win on this turn, do so.
> Else if the opponent is about to win, block him.
> Else if you can achieve a fork, do so.
> Else if you can prevent the opponent from creating a fork, do so.
> Else move in the "best" square possible, where the center beats the corner which beats the side.

Suppose, though, the instructions for such a game were not given verbally, but in the form of pictures of board configurations. This is a perfectly legitimate and equivalent instruction set. It is now difficult to imagine that someone who plays game after game by matching configuration diagrams would not after time begin to get the hang of the rules, to the extent that he would be able to take over and play well without the instructions at all. What is happening during the transition period is that the instructions for the game are being internalized, in other words compiled. The transition from interpretation to compilation represents the generation of some level of understanding. The fact that the player does not know he is playing tic-tac-toe does not mean the exercise is carried out without intensionality, since natural human teleological tendencies will cause intensionality to be ascribed to the symbols themselves.

Turing was of the opinion[24] that building a learning machine was preferable to building a machine that was initially intelligent: [25]

> If we are trying to produce an intelligent machine, and are following the human model as closely as we can, we should begin with a machine with very little capacity to carry out elaborate operations or to react in a disciplined manner to orders (taking the form of interference). Then by applying appropriate interference, mimicking education, we should hope to modify the machine until it could be relied on to produce definite reactions to certain commands. This would be the beginning of the process.

Summary

Understanding is not an atomic phenomenon, and exists in varying levels or degrees, even with respect to simple facts and objects. Understanding in humans exists at both the cognitive and subcognitive levels. This has been modelled in computers, in the former case by AI programs such as expert systems and theorem-provers that use inference engines, facts and rules, and in the latter case by connectionist, neural-network models.[26] Two related phenomena, however, which would seem to be essential for any complete model of understanding, still await adequate treatment, both theoretically and in practical models. These are (1) thinking systems that employ both cognitive and sub-cognitive functionality, and allow smooth switching between them, or of introspection of one by the other, and (2) the act of transition from cognitive to sub-cognitive. Something weird and wonderful happens when we learn a skill; at one moment we are conscious of the steps we are taking as we carefully follow the rules we have been taught, and the next we have "grokked"[27] the task and can act "on automatic". It is not unreasonable to suppose that when these problems have been solved, machines can be expected to approach Turing test capability, and objections such as Searle's will melt away.

Searle argues that a program cannot be intelligent if it doesn't have intensionality, but it is difficult to see what he would accept as proof in the case that a program does. The related argument that a program cannot be intelligent without emotions, falls flat because there is no reason why emotions cannot be quantified (at least their result if not their cause). This reasoning would seem to degenerate to the simplistic argument that flesh-and-blood is required for intelligence, which in turn becomes the "Heads in the Sand" argument from *Computing Machinery and Intelligence*. We will leave the last word to Turing. In the earlier paper *Intelligent Machinery* (1948), part of which could be considered a draft of *Computing Machinery and Intelligence*, he had included a reason others might object to machine intelligence:

> An unwillingness to admit the possibility that mankind can have any rivals in intellectual power. This occurs as much among intellectual people as amongst others: they have more to lose. Those who admit the possibility all agree that its realization would be very disagreeable. The same situation arises in connection with the possibility of our being superseded by some other animal species. This is almost as disagreeable and its theoretical possibility is indisputable.

Endnotes

[1] Some other programs work in the reverse order: the desired conclusion is posed as a goal and the program proceeds to prove it as a necessary conclusion from the given facts, much like the operation of the plane geometry theorem-provers.

[2] Penrose (1989).

[3] Penrose himself suggests that some kind of quantum-mechanical effects are involved here.

[4] Dreyfus (1979).

[5] Edelman (1992) p. 147. The book as a whole addresses the emergence of the mind in the brain.

---

[6] Searle (1980).

[7] Schank and Abelson (1977).

[8] While in the early days of artificial intelligence researchers were primarily concerned with computational processes, they became increasingly aware of the importance of the format in which the internal data that AI programs used to guide those computations was stored. This is the problem of *knowledge representation*, and remains one of the principal fields of AI research today. Schank's scripts were one particular knowledge representation format, designed to help explore the issues of understanding within a predefined context. An approximately parallel development was that of *frames*, by Minsky (1975). Other formalisms, such as predicate logic and semantic networks, amongst others, have been proposed and used with varying success in (usually small) AI prototypes. Interestingly, brain researchers are less far along. Some of the computational properties of the neural system are partially understood, but so far any real progress in understanding how knowledge is stored in the brain has remained elusive. Taking words as an example, it is not known whether words are stored associated with concepts or concepts with words. The granularity of neural substrate used (as distinct from necessary) for representation is also unknown; is one neuron used per word, are several necessary, or are several words stored per neuron – or are words stored in a distributed, holographic manner?

[9] Dennett (1991), p. 436.

[10] Chapter 22, section "Reflections", in Hofstadter & Dennett (1981).

[11] Turing (1948), p. 13.

[12] According to legend, the problem originated in a monastery in the far East, where monks were obliged to move large stone discs according to the problem specifications as part of their daily rituals.

[13] Reah. ©1998 by LK Avalon, published by Project Two Interactive BV.

[14] Turing (1953).

[15] Hodges (1983).

[16] known in England as draughts.

[17] A game that involves taking sticks from piles, the loser being the one left with the last stick.

[18] Samuel (1959).

[19] Experienced programmers will note that we have taken some liberties here in order to avoid complicating the exposition needlessly.

[20] To get a computer to generate a working program from the English description would be a challenging task for an AI programmer; if the computer could see examples of solved problems for various values of N the task would be a degree easier.

[21] It is straightforward, for a skilled programmer at least, to program a computer to successfully perform these tasks; however this is not what we are asking. We are asking whether a computer just programmed to solve the original problem would be able to solve these auxiliary problems as a direct consequence of its initial programming.

[22] Michie (1974) p. 122-3 discusses some of the ambiguity in these lines.

[23] This phrase comes from the time when political candidates would campaign in horse-drawn wagons, and those wishing to demonstrate their support would climb on board. There is nothing special about this example; there are doubtless thousands of other examples that would serve just as well.

[24] Turing (1948) p. 14.

[25] Not that he or anyone since has achieved a truly intelligent machine by either route. Early attempts at building machines which exhibit intelligent natural-language dialogue, when restricted to certain domains, have attracted much attention. Examples include Weizenbaum's (1966) ELIZA which mimicked a therapist by using certain tricks, such as throwing the patient's comments back at him ("Why did you say you didn't like your teacher?"), and Colby's (1973) PARRY, which explored belief systems in the form of a simulated paranoid patient. Machine learning has been a *bona fide* subfield of artificial intelligence for many years, using techniques from the symbolic to the statistical, inductive to analytic. For a good text on this subject, see Mitchell (1997).

[26] Neural network modelling essentially began with the idealized neurons of McCulloch and Pitts (1943), and continued with the Perceptrons of Rosenblatt (1962). The field foundered somewhat after it was shown that Perceptrons couldn't even simulate the exclusive-or function of Boolean logic. However, with the back-propagation algorithm of Rumelhart and McClelland (1986), the field of connectionism took off and is today considered a quite respectable approach to the problem of machine learning.

[27] The term invented by Robert A. Heinlein and used in *Stranger in a Strange Land* to describe the experience of fully comprehending a new concept.

7
Concluding Remarks

In preparation for this book, a Web search was performed using names of 20th century philosophers and scientists. In terms of numbers of pages found, *Turing* came in second only to *Einstein.*[1] Obviously such a popularity contest is not a strict determiner of importance, but it does give an indication of the extent to which the contributions of Alan Turing are recognized in the world today.

In the fields of mathematical logic and computer science, Turing has lent his name to the (Church-)Turing Thesis, the Turing machine and the Turing test, all of which have been discussed at length in this book. Monetary prizes have been offered for systems that could pass the Turing test. The Association for Computing Machinery (ACM), the premier professional society for computer scientists, has named its prestigious annual prize the Turing Award, the winner of which delivers the Turing Award Lecture. In Glasgow, Scotland, there is the Turing Institute, which conducts research into artificial intelligence.

Alan Turing was the founder of modern computing, programming, software engineering, artificial intelligence – or so it has been claimed at one time or another. While this obviously overstates the case, it is true that success has many parents and Turing is at the very least an uncle or grandfather of these fields.

Despite such recognition, Turing never reached the very peak of his career professionally. When he died he was a Fellow of the Royal Society and on the staff of Manchester University. Had he lived he could conceivably have achieved a chair at Cambridge. Had they been awarded during World War II he might have won the Fields medal.[2]

Whatever one considers the year of the "big bang" that started the era of electronic computers, in Turing's time the radius of that universe was still small enough that one man could manage to embrace it all, and if any man did, that man was Alan Turing.. Not only did he work in and publish in fields from philosophy to engineering, but he made such significant contributions that his work is still being discussed.

Alan Turing's name is unfortunately not widely recognized in the non-scientific population at large, and even amongst computer professionals his accomplishments are not as appreciated as they might be. However, there is one sense in which his name crops up continually in comments made by practitioners in the field. When we buy software for our personal computers we have to give consideration to which packages run on which machines. The ability of a certain piece of software to run or not on a given machine is not a *necessary* consequence of the design of the hardware or the software, but a consequence of a variety of incidental or exogenous criteria – be they economical, aesthetic, competitive or pragmatic – in the minds of the authors or publishers. *In practice* a particular program might not run on a particular computer, but *in principle* there is no reason why it cannot – after all, "the computer is just a Turing machine."

Endnotes

[1] This little experiment was done on May 27, 2000 using the search engine at http://www.altavista.com. The numbers of pages found for the top 10 names were as follows (including matches for common misspellings): Einstein 247,675; Turing 49,950; Planck (but not the Institute) 44,690; Wittgenstein 42,930; Hilbert 39,795; Schrödinger 38,128; Bohr 37,680; Heisenberg 36,430; von Neumann 30,961; Dirac 28,647. Clearly this is not an accurate test since overcounting will occur from matching other individuals with the same names, although all the names tried are relatively unusual. On the other hand, people who name their pet goldfish, for example, with any of these can be assumed to be paying tribute to the so-named philosopher or scientist. This demonstration should not be taken too seriously.

[2] There is no Nobel Prize in mathematics. The most coveted award in the field is the Fields Medal, awarded by the International Congress of Mathematicians in Toronto to recognize outstanding mathematics achievement. It is awarded every four years, and the winners must be less than 40 years of age.

References

The *Collected Works of A.M. Turing* is available in four volumes from North-Holland press:
Pure Mathematics, edited by J.L Britton,
Mathematical Logic, edited by R.O. Gandy and C.E.M. Yates,
Mechanical Intelligence, edited by D.C. Ince, and
Morphogenesis, edited by P.T. Saunders.

For an excellent and very comprehensive biography, see:

Hodges, Andrew (1983). *Alan Turing: the Enigma*, Simon and Schuster, New York.
Hodges also has a very informative web-site about Turing at http://www.turing.org.uk/turing/

Other References

Colby, K.M. (1973). "Simulations of Belief Systems". In R.C Schank and K.M. Colby (Eds.) *Computer Models of Thought and Language*, W.H. Freeman & Co., San Francisco.

Collins, H.M. (1990). *Artificial Experts*, MIT Press, Cambridge, MA.

Dennett, D.C. (1991). *Consciousness Explained*, Little Brown & Co., Boston.

Dreyfus, H. (1979). *What Computers Can't Do: The Limits of Artificial Intelligence*. New York, Harper and Row.

Dyson, G.B. (1997). *Darwin among the Machines*, Perseus Books.

References

Edelman, G.M. (1992). *Bright Air, Brilliant Fire*, Basic Books.

Gödel, K (1931). "Über formal unentscheidbare Sätze der Principia Mathematica und verwandter Systeme I", *Monatshefte für Mathematik und Physik*, **38**, pp 173-198.

Hinsley, F.H. and Stripp, A. (editors) (1993). *Codebreakers: The Inside Story of Bletchley Park*, Oxford University Press, Oxford.

Greene, B.R. (1999). *The Elegant Universe*, Norton & Co., New York.

Hintikka, J. (2000). *Gödel*, Wadsworth.

Hofstadter, D. R. (1979). *Gödel, Escher, Bach: an Eternal Golden Braid*, Basic Books, New York.

Hofstadter, D.R. & Dennett, D.C. (1981). *The Mind's I*, Bantam Books, New York.

Hopcroft, J.E. and Ullman, J.D. (1979). *Introduction to Automata Theory, Languages and Computation*, Addison-Wesley, Reading, MA.

Kleene, S.C. (1936). "General recursive functions of natural numbers", *Math. Annalen 112*, pp. 340-353.

Lavington, S. (1980). *Early British Computers*, Digital Press, Bedford, MA.

McCulloch, W.S. and Pitts, W. (1943). "A logical calculus of the ideas immanent in nervous activity", *Bulletin of Mathematical Biophysics* **5**, pp. 115-133.

Michie, D. (1974). *On Machine Intelligence*, John Wiley & Sons, New York.

Minsky, M.L. (1972). *Computation: Finite and Infinite Machines*, Prentice-Hall International, London.

Minsky, M.L. (1975). "A framework for representing knowledge." In P. H. Winston (Ed.), *The Psychology of Computer Vision* pp. 211-277, McGraw-Hill, New York.

Minsky, M. & Papert, S. (1969). *Perceptrons*. MIT Press, Cambridge, MA.

Mitchell, T.M. (1997). *Machine Learning*, McGraw-Hill, New York.

81

Penrose, R. (1989). *The Emperor's New Mind. Concerning Computers, Minds and the Laws of Physics*, Penguin, New York.

Post, E.L. (1943). "Formal reductions of the general combinatorial decision problem", *Am. Journal of Math. 65*, pp. 197-268.

Randell, B. (Editor) (1973). *The Origins of Digital Computers*, Spreinger-Verlag, Berlin.

Rosenblatt, F. (1962). *Principles of Neurodynamics*, Spartan, New York.

Rumelhart, D.E. and McClelland, J.L. (1986). *Parallel Distributed Computing*, MIT Press, Cambridge, MA.

Samuel, A.L. (1959). "Some studies in machine learning using the game of checkers", *IBM J. Res. Dev. 3*, pp.211-229.

Schank, R.C. and Abelson, R.P. (1977). *Scripts, Plans, Goals and Understanding*, Erlbaum, Hillsdale, N.J.

Searle, J.R. (1980). "Minds, Brains, and Programs," *The Behavioral and Brain Sciences, vol. 3.* Cambridge University Press.

Shannon, C.E. (1956). "A universal Turing machine with two internal states", *Automata Studies (Annals of Math. Studies 34)*, Princeton.

Turing, A.M. (1937). "On computable numbers, with an application to the Entscheidungsproblem", *Proc. London Math. Soc., Ser(2)* **42**, pp. 230-265.

Turing, A.M. (1945). "Proposals for Development in the Mathematics Division of an Automatic Computing Engine (ACE)." Report to the Executive Committee of the National Physics Laboratory. In: B.E. Carpenter and R.N. Doran (Editors), *A.M. Turing's ACE Report of 1946 and Other Papers* (MIT Press, Cambridge, MA, 1986) Chapter 2, pp. 2-105.

Turing, A.M. (1947). Lecture to the London Mathematical Society on 20 February 1947. In: B.E. Carpenter and R.N. Doran (Editors), *A.M. Turing's ACE Report of 1946 and Other Papers* (MIT Press, Cambridge, MA, 1986) Chapter 3, pp. 106-124.

Turing, A.M. (1948). "Intelligent Machinery". Report, National Physical Laboratory. In: B. Meltzer and D. Michie (Editors), *Machine Intelligence 5*, Edinburgh, pp. 3-23.

References

Turing, A.M. (1950). "Computing Machinery and Intelligence", *MIND LIX*, pp. 433-460.

Turing, A.M. (1953). "Digital Computers Applied to Games", in B.V. Bowden (editor), *Faster than Thought*, Pitman, London, pp. 286-310.

Weizenbaum, J. (1966). "ELIZA -- A computer program for the study of natural language communication between man and machine", *Communications of the ACM 9(1)*: pp. 36-45.